GO
&
AND A NIGHTIN

Good, with Alan Howard playing Halder, was premièred by the Royal Shakespeare Company at their London Warehouse in September 1981.

'Taylor's play is about moral compromise in a political fog, and like all good plays is as much about now as then'.

Snoo Wilson, *Time Out*

And a Nightingale Sang . . . was written for the Live Theatre group and first staged in Newcastle in March 1977.

'Every once in a while the theatre produces an evening so unexpected, so instantly recognizable as the stuff of humanity, that it rocks you back in your seat'.

Daily Mail

C P Taylor, born in Glasgow in 1929, was a prolific writer both for theatre and television, and he was closely associated with the Newcastle group, the Live Theatre Company, for which he wrote *And a Nightingale Sang* . . . *Good* was premièred by the Royal Shakespeare Company at the Warehouse in 1981, and was instantly greeted as a tour de force. His other plays published by Methuen include *Peter Pan Man, The Black and White Minstrels, Gynt!, You are My Heart's Delight, To be a Farmer's Boy* and *Bring Me Sunshine, Bring Me Smiles*. They are available in one volume, entitled *North*. Cecil Taylor died in December 1981.

A METHUEN MODERN PLAY

This edition first published in 1990 by Methuen Drama,
215 Vauxhall Bridge Road, London SW1V 1EJ

10 9 8 7 6 5 4 3

This collection Copyright © 1990 by the Estate of the late Cecil P Taylor

Good first published in Great Britain in 1982 by Methuen London Ltd.
Reprinted 1982
Revised, reset and first published in Great Britain and U.S.A. 1983
Copyright © 1982, 1990 by Cecil P Taylor.

And a Nightingale Sang . . . first published in Great Britain in 1979 by Eyre
Methuen Ltd
Reprinted 1983 and 1984 by Methuen London Ltd
Copyright © 1979, 1990 by Cecil P Taylor.

A CIP catalogue record for this book is available from the British Library
ISBN 0 413 63910 X

Printed and bound in Great Britain by
Cox & Wyman Ltd, Reading, Berkshire

The photograph on the front cover is by Alastair Muir and shows Alan Howard
as Halder, Pip Miller as Freddie and Chris Hunter as Hitler in the 1981 RSC
Warehouse production.
The photograph of Cecil Taylor on the back cover is by George Oliver.

CAUTION

All rights in these plays are strictly reserved and application for performance
etc should be made before rehearsal to: Alan Brodie Representation,
211 Piccadilly, London W1V 9LD.

Good

A Tragedy

**In memory of my father
Max George Taylor
A refugee from anti-Semitism
in Czarist Russia**

Good was first presented at the RSC Warehouse, London, on 2 September 1981, with the following cast:

HALDER	Alan Howard
SISTER	Penelope Beaumont
MOTHER	Barbara Kinghorn
DOCTOR	Timothy Walker
MAURICE	Joe Melia
HELEN	Domini Blythe
BOULLER	Nicholas Woodeson
ANNE	Felicity Dean
FREDDIE	Pip Miller
HITLER	Chris Hunter
BOK	Chris Hunter
ELISABETH	Penelope Beaumont
DESPATCH RIDER	Timothy Walker
EICHMANN	Nicholas Woodeson

Musicians:

PIANO/ACCORDIAN	Nigel Hess
VIOLIN	Alastair McLachlan
SAXOPHONE/CLARINET	Victor Slaymark
BANJO/GUITAR	George Weigand
TRUMPET	Roderick Tearle

Directed by Howard Davies
Designs by Ultz
Lighting by Michael Calf
Music arranged by George Fenton
Musical Director Nigel Hess
Sound by John A. Leonard

This production transferred to the Aldwych Theatre, London, on 22 April 1982, with the following changes of cast:

SISTER/ELISABETH	Gay Soper
DOCTOR/DESPATCH RIDER	Benedick Blythe
HITLER/BOK	David Howey

Musicians
Roger Hellyer, Alastair McLachlan, Alan Andrews, George Weigand, Colin Rae

At the time of going to press, the RSC production of *Good* was scheduled to open at the Booth Theatre on Broadway in October 1982, with the following changes of cast:

HELEN	Megwyn Owen
MOTHER	Margorie Yates
DOCTOR/DESPATCH RIDER	Timothy Walker
NURSE/ELISABETH	Kate Spiro
MAURICE	Gary Waldhorn

Author's Note

Although *Good* is obviously based on facts of recent history, documentary material, and is peopled in some cases by real characters, this story of how a 'good' man gets caught up in the nightmare of the Third Reich is a work of the imagination.

What the tragedy which I have written as a comedy, or *musical-comedy* is about, will hopefully emerge in the performance. If it proves the good play we hope it is, like all good plays, it will have a special meaning, or shade of meaning, for each person who experiences it.

The writing of the play is my response to a deeply felt, and deeply experienced trauma in recent history, the Third Reich's war on the Jews, as well as an intellectual awareness, not at all deeply felt, of my role as a 'Peace Criminal' in the Peace 'Crimes' of the West against the Third World — my part in the Auschwitzes we are all perpetrating today.

I put 'crimes' in inverted commas, because my concept of history — which will hopefully emerge from the play — is not quite simple enought to allow me to see either the anti-social activities of the Third Reich, or of the West today, as simply criminal. If the problem were so simple, the solution might then be equally so.

I grew up during the war under a deeply felt anxiety that the Germans might win the war, overrun Britain and that I and my mother and father would end up, like my less fortunate co-religionists, in a Nazi Death Camp — perhaps specially built in Scotland or England.

There seems to have been some pressure building up in me for a long time to write a play about the Final Solution, marking and responding to a great historical and personal trauma. Not as a Jew, wanting to add my wreath to those already piled high at the graves of the Six Million, but as my own little gesture to revive their memory in our consciousness. It still seems that there are lessons to be learned if we can examine the atrocities of the Third Reich as the result of the infinite complexity of contemporary human society, and not a simple conspiracy of criminals and psychopaths. The 'Inhumanities' seem to me only too human and leading to a final Final Solution to end all Final Solutions — the solution to the Human Problem, a nuclear holocaust.

C.P. Taylor

Act One

Thirties dance band ensemble. The band is playing: 'I'm Always Chasing Rainbows'.

HALDER (*to the audience*). The bands came in 1933. So you can't say they came with the rise of the Nazis, exactly. The Nazis were on the rise long before that. To some extent, it was a device that was with me from childhood. Bringing music into the dramatic moments of my life. But from '33, they became an addiction. Jazz bands . . . café bands . . . tenors . . . crooners . . . symphony orchestras . . . Depending on the particular situation and my mood.

A strategy for survival? Turning the reality into fantasy?

It was a dance band, that day. What they were playing was an English song — or an American. Is there any difference?

SISTER (*impatiently*). Doctor Halder?

HALDER. Yes. I'm coming.

The CROONER *is into the middle section.*

CROONER. Why should I always be a failure? Why should I never get the breaks?

HALDER (*to the audience*). Stolen, of course, from Chopin . . . *Fantasie Impromptu* . . . Nice, wallowing-in self-pity kind of thing.

HALDER *and the band approach the* SISTER.

SISTER. Visiting hours are between seven and eight, Doctor Halder.

HALDER. I live in Frankfurt, you see . . .

SISTER. I see.

HALDER. Long journey to Hamburg . . . Busy time at the University, just now. Coming up to examinations.

SISTER. You can go and see her for ten minutes or so. But we are about to serve lunch.

MOTHER *is wheeled towards* HALDER *in an invalid chair.*

MOTHER. Johnnie. Listen to me. Get me out of here. Another day, and I'll go out of my mind. Get a chair for Helen. (*To where she imagines* HELEN *is:*) Helen, have pity on me.

HALDER. Helen's not there, Mother . . . (*The band is about to play again.* HALDER *waves them away. They put down their instruments.*)

MOTHER. Will you get your wife a chair. This isn't the time or place for jokes, son.

HALDER. Mother, you're imagining it. She's not here.

MOTHER. She's not standing beside you?

HALDER. It's just you're confused, just now. That's all.

MOTHER. Listen, are you trying to make me mad altogether? Helen, tell him. He has to get me out of here . . . Have pity on me.

HALDER. You've been in a coma, mother. A thyroid deficiency . . . one of the effects . . . you see things.

MOTHER. Helen's not there? Are you not there, Helen? Wait a minute. Do you think I'm going out of my mind? If I'm going out of my mind . . . that's a bad business.

HALDER. It makes you confused . . . That's all.

MOTHER. Wait a minute. Last night. Did that happen? You were drunk . . . and banging at the door all night to get in?

HALDER. Imagination.

MOTHER. John . . . Come closer to me, a minute. (*Looking round to make sure nobody's listening.*) Is anybody listening to us?

HALDER. No one is near us . . .

MOTHER (*whispering*). You're not a communist?

HALDER. You know that. I could never accept Marxism. Parts of it . . . yes.

MOTHER. I'm *talking* to you, son. You're not a communist and Hitler's not going to put you in prison. Your trial's this afternoon.

HALDER. For God's sake, mother!

MOTHER. Oh, thank God . . . Thank God . . . You're *not*?

HALDER. Mother!

MOTHER. Listen . . . I'm going out of my mind . . . Johnnie, I've got to go home.

HALDER. You can't *see*, mother.

MOTHER. What about your house?

HALDER. With the children and Helen . . . I couldn't cope with you, mother. *I* would . . . but how can I ask the children and Helen . . .

MOTHER. Listen. Is that my imagination too? This place, it's a *front*. Men come up here to go with the women . . . That sister, there . . .

HALDER. This hospital's a front for a brothel?

MOTHER. Is it not? . . . Johnnie, this is a bad business . . . I'm going out of my mind . . .

HALDER. I could cope with you for a *week*, mother . . . We'd *like* to have you for a week or so . . . But you know what Helen's like. She can't even organise the house with just *us* in it . . . You wouldn't be happy . . . You never are there . . .

MOTHER. The best thing is to take twenty or thirty of my pills and finish myself off once and for all . . .

HALDER. You could do that. It's against the law, but . . .

MOTHER. What have I got to live for? I can't see. My eyes are finished. Nobody wants me . . . I'm better out of it . . . What have I got to live for, for God's sake!

HALDER (*looks round . . . lost . . .*). A difficult question, that.

A CLERK comes to him.

CLERK. Can I help you?

HALDER. This *is* Tiergartenstrasse Four? . . . I'm looking for the Committee for Research into Hereditary Diseases . . . Over-Leader Philip Bouller . . .

CLERK. You've come down the wrong passage . . . I'll show you where his office is, Herr . . .

HALDER. Professor Halder . . . Is this some new committee . . . ? I've never heard of it before.

CLERK. It's just been set up, Herr Professor . . . You have an appointment with the Over-Leader?

HALDER. I have an appointment. Yes . . . Pleasant place . . . To work in.

CLERK. Professor . . . It used to be one of the best residential areas in Berlin. Charlottenburg . . . I'll see if the Over-Leader is free Herr Professor . . . (*He goes.*)

HALDER *paces up and down waiting.*

MAURICE. Will you stop bloody wandering around, man. Sit down . . . *Bands*?

HALDER. Have you *got* to be a doctor, Maurice?

MAURICE. I *am* a doctor. It's an automatic response. Somebody comes to me as a doctor. I'm a doctor. Listen. What do you want to do? Pull me into *your* neurosis? I've got my own, thanks.

HALDER. Maurice, how could I come to you as a doctor, for God's sake? The question I am putting to you — as my closest friend. (*To the audience*:) My *only* friend. (*To* MAURICE:) Should I see a psychiatrist?

MAURICE. *Bands*?

HALDER. Music, generally. Not very big bands. Odd times, the Berlin Philharmonic . . . Last Senate meeting, it was the Phil. Playing the Storm Movement from The Pastoral . . .

Not just the bands, Maurice . . . I want to try and throw off this neurosis I've been living with all my life . . . To give my work and my family relationships a more healthy basis . . .

MAURICE. What does *that* mean? That's *words*, Johnnie. Johnnie . . . That's verbal shit you're giving me . . . *We* don't work like that, for Christ's sake! *You* and *me*.

HALDER. I want to *try*. All my work so far has been based on this bloody anxiety neurosis. I do. I want to see what work I can do, free of it.

MAURICE. What's he talking about? What's this man talking about? People don't go to analysts to streamline their lives . . . They go to free themselves from agony. Listen, I know. You're suffering . . . You have to tell me about it. I'm your friend for Christ's sake . . .

. . . Just now . . . If you want to know about suffering . . . My agony, just now . . . My neuritic track . . . That wakes me up four o'clock in the morning in a panic . . .

HALDER. I can't get *lost* you see? I can't lose myself in people or situations. Everything's acted out against this bloody musical background.

MAURICE. *Objectively. Intellectually* . . . The Nazis . . . That's just flag-waving to get hold of the masses . . . This anti-Jew hysteria . . . Now it's got them where they wanted to go . . .

HALDER. Could it be some sub-conscious comment on my loose grip of reality? The whole of my life is a performance? Is that too glib, do you think, Maurice?

MAURICE. If you knew the unconscious like I do . . . Nothing's too glib for that bastard. What I'm saying to you . . . Listen to me . . . It's interesting, sometimes, listening to other people . . . You don't need to make too big a habit of it . . . but odd times . . .

HALDER. I'm *listening*.

MAURICE. I'm telling you . . . I know, for Christ's sake . . . The Nazis are politicians above everything else. Realists . . . I know that . . .

CLERK (*coming to* HALDER): Professor Halder?

HALDER. I'm slightly early. I can never time appointments. I'm sorry.

CLERK. Over-Leader Bouller has someone with him at present. He will see you shortly.

HALDER. That's all right. That's fine. I have my book here . . . This is a new committee . . . I gather . . .

CLERK (going). You will have to excuse me. Heil Hitler . . .

HALDER. Yes, of course. Heil Hitler . . . (Political gesture.)

MAURICE. Politicians are practical people. I know that. They're realists . . . They live in the world as it is . . .

HALDER. Let's just have some coffee, Maurice. Forget about my problems.

MAURICE. Listen. Is it sex, Johnnie? I'm asking is it sex . . . Of course it's sex . . . Everything's sex . . . Sex is very difficult, Johnnie . . . I don't personally know anybody who doesn't find sex difficult, Johnnie . . . If that's any comfort . . . Listen . . . If it's potency problems . . . Or maybe some taste you've developed . . . Bondage, for example . . . That's no problem if you can find somebody with mutual interests . . . Or tranvestism . . . You'd be amazed how common tranvestism is . . .

HALDER. I've never been attracted to bondage or flogging or anything like that, Maurice . . . Probably, my sexual imagination is very limited . . .

MAURICE. Listen, I know how much Germany depends on Jewish brains . . . Jewish business . . . Hitler's got all the power he needs now. They're bound to drop all that racial shit they had to throw around to get their votes . . . They can't afford not to. I know that . . . But I can't believe it.

You see what I'm getting at . . . I'm sorry . . . I'm developing an obsession . . . I'm in a bloody panic state . . . Look at me . . .

HALDER. I'll get you a drink, Maurice . . . Relax . . . You're right . . . All that anti-Jew rubbish . . . You're right . . . Just balloons they throw up in the air to distract the masses . . . You're right.

MAURICE. I *know* I'm bloody right. I'm telling you . . . But my blood anxiety neurosis has fixed on to it . . . and I can do shit all about it . . . Listen . . . What do I want to run off to England for . . . Or Shanghai . . .

HALDER. Shanghai might be interesting. China . . .

MAURICE. This is my home. I love Frankfurt. I love Hessen. I love the whole bloody place . . .

HALDER. Take a bit of cheesecake, Maurice.

MAURICE. I'm a German. I was born here. Look at me. I don't look Jewish. It could well be my grandmother had it off with some Bavarian peasant or plumber or something . . . Who the bloody hell knows . . .

HALDER. Maurice . . . You're right . . . The racialist programme is not practical . . . They'll drop it . . . They'll have to drop it . . .

MAURICE. I said I *know* I'm right . . . I *know* . . . *I* don't want any cheesecake. This is my *home* . . . Every morning . . . Before breakfast . . . I take a walk in Nizza Park . . . Along the river . . .

HALDER. Yes . . . You're right . . . talking about impotence complexes . . . I might have a bit of . . .

MAURICE. I'm telling you about my feelings for Frankfurt . . . ! Walking about Frankfurt in the morning. Looking at the river and the trees . . . and the wonderful buildings. The *pride*. For Christ's sake . . . You are . . . You're proud to be a German . . . To live in a city like this . . . Walking by the cathedral . . .

HALDER (*to himself*): He's a nice man. I love him. But I cannot get involved with his problems. So in the next few months they might kick in his teeth. But just now, he's all right. What's he worried about? I bet you *he* has no problems in bed with his wife. *I've* got problems *now*. *Me*. My problem is *immediate*. It's an urgent problem . . .

(*To* MAURICE:) You're right Maurice. It's a beautiful city to live in.

MAURICE. Was that you having a visitation from one of your bands just now?

HALDER. I do that from time to time. I talk to myself in my mind. That's another addiction.

MAURICE. About me?

HALDER. More or less.

MAURICE. Negative — resentment?

HALDER. Negative *and* positive, Maurice.

MAURICE. This morning . . . Walking along Deer's Ditch . . . Passing Goethe's house . . . I thought about you. What a worthwhile man that is . . . Johnnie Halder . . . Good! I love him.

HALDER. You know Goethe refused to send Beethoven money when he was desperate . . . Dying . . .

MAURICE. Listen. Don't talk about Beethoven, Johnnie . . .

HALDER. I never knew that till a few weeks ago. The week Hitler became Chancellor, I happened to be going through some papers in the library . . . I found this letter . . . Beethoven writing to Goethe for a few marks . . . Desperate . . . Last days before he died. The swine wouldn't send him a penny! Ignored his letter . . .

MAURICE (*watching* HALDER — *sudden insight*). Do you know what's happened? It's just come to me John . . . Hitler has perverted the whole nature of our relationship. Buggered up one of the few friendships I valued . . . That's not *good*, Johnnie.

HALDER (*to himself*): Failing. I don't like failing . . . Failing throws me into a panic state . . . It's not good.

MAURICE. I'm envious . . . I'm bloody envious.

HALDER. Of my *state*, Maurice?

MAURICE. You're *safe*. That's what I'm talking about. You can stay in Frankfurt for the rest of your life. End up Professor — Vice-chancellor . . . *I* cannot predict what pillow I'll be resting my head on tonight . . .

HALDER. That's panicking, Maurice. That really is.

MAURICE. It is . . . You're right. Next *week*.

HALDER. Maurice, we've established that . . . They've got to drop the Anti-Jew programme . . . In the long run . . . For the survival of the bloody state . . .

MAURICE. *I* know that . . . and *you* know that . . . But does bloody *Hitler* . . . That's what's worrying me . . . That's it — not neurosis at all . . . It's bloody reality . . .

HALDER. The night the girl turned up at my house, I turned it into an opera . . . There was a Café Trio . . . Playing Wagner . . .

Café trio playing 'Star of Eve' from 'Tannhäuser'.

HALDER (*stepping over the debris of his living-room . . . To the audience*): I had difficulties stepping through the debris of Helen's battle with the day . . . Helen was lying in front of the fire reading a biography of Telemann, waiting for me to cook the supper for the kids . . .

(*To the accompaniement of the trio: Recitativo to* HELEN:)

> I bought some smoked ham,
> Panhas and bread.
> You need not trouble,
> Your pretty head.
> Everything's cold,
> No need to wait,
> Just take your seat,
> And fill your plate.

HELEN (*recitativo*):

> Darling, I want to talk to you seriously.
> Your mother 'phoned,
> Very disturbing.
> And my father,
> We had a long conversation.
> I hate nagging at you,
> But really you can't hang on any longer.
> You'll have to shake yourself,
> Out of this apathy.

HALDER (*with the food, recitativo*):
>Will you have it at the fire,
>If I clear the newspapers
>And scores?
>I think I can get down to the carpet.
>I quite like eating on the floor.

HELEN (*recitativo*):
>I had mother pick up the children,
>From school and take them home for a meal.

HALDER (*recitativo*):
>Should we try a maid,
>Once more.
>I know you find it hard
>Having strangers living with us.

HELEN. Johnnie . . . I'm useless . . . I spent all afternoon trying to play these triplets against crochets in that Beethoven sonata . . . My whole life . . . Everything . . .

Look at the state this house is in. I didn't even clean my teeth this morning. I'm a slut. I've no idea why you love me. *Do* you, love?

HALDER. Yes. I love you.

CLERK. Over-Leader Bouller will see you now, Herr Professor.

HALDER. Thank you. (*Going to* BOULLER.) Heil Hitler.

BOULLER. Heil Hitler. Please sit down, Herr Professor . . . Make yourself comfortable . . . Please if you wish to smoke, be at ease to do so.

HALDER. Thank you, Over-Leader . . . I don't smoke . . .

BOULLER. Before we begin, I wish this to be clearly understood. Everything that is discussed between us in this room is absolutely Top Secret. This is understood?

HALDER. Absolutely, Over-Leader . . .

BOULLER. Apart from knowing something of your work and your record since you joined us, your superiors have recommended you without reservation as a person of total loyalty to the state and National Socialism.

... Would you consider this an accurate description of your
position and commitment?

HALDER. I've written about this, Over-Leader ... I am
committed to use whatever abilities and talents I might have
for the betterment of the lives of the people round me ...

BOULLER. Are you warm, Herr Professor? It's a hot day.

HALDER. Slightly ... Yes.

BOULLER. Please ... Take your jacket off ... Make yourself
comfortable ... We have called you here in the role of a
consultant ... A comrade who we can trust and who is, at the
same time, something of a figure in the academic world ...

We have been reading your novel ... As you see ... About life
in a home for the aged ... You raise very interesting moral
questions in it, Herr Halder ... Some of your conclusions
... *Fascinating* ... *Profoundly* ...

HALDER. It was a subject close to me ... at the time ...

BOULLER. I have coffee at two-thirty. Would you like coffee?

HALDER. Please ... Yes ...

BOULLER. I'll arrange to have an extra cup brought in ... In
the meantime, this is a letter I would like you to read. It
was sent direct to the Chancellory for the attention of The
Leader ... It's from the father of a deformed child ...
(*Going.*) Even your wife, Herr Professor ... Not a *hint* of
what is discussed here must be communicated to even your
wife ... Not a word ... This is a direct order from the top
Leadership ... You understand this ... ?

HALDER. Fully, Over-Leader ... Yes ...

HELEN (*calling to him*): John, I'm sorry ...

HALDER. Why should you be sorry? I don't mind living in
chaos. It's all right. The children are used to it.

HELEN. You come back from a hard day at work, and I
overwhelm you with self-pity ...

HALDER. Yes.

HELEN. You shouldn't stand this. Me turning your house into a shithouse, Johnnie.

HALDER. Tell you what. After tea, we'll clean it up.

HELEN (*with a pastry*). I wish you wouldn't buy these pastries. It's just indulging my greed and making me fat . . .

HALDER. Don't eat them.

HELEN. For Christ's sake, why do you love me?

HALDER. I don't know why I love you. Have you got to?

HELEN. I can't even look after your bloody kids . . . Father rang . . .

HALDER (*to the audience*): Behaviourist psychiatrist . . . Losing clients left, right and centre to Jewish Freudians . . . All right now, Hitler was in . . .

HELEN. He wants to speak to you. Tonight. He says the time is long past for being pure and self-righteous. For the sake of your children and me . . . You must make a definite decision to join the National Socialists . . . With your army record, they'll welcome you with open arms . . .

. . . Actually, he heard from somebody very high up, Goebbels has read your *Faust and Goethe in Weimar* . . .

HALDER. I was thinking about Hitler, on my way home.

HELEN. He's right. You'll get nowhere in the university now, unless you join the party, Johnnie . . . Father says you could even lose your lectureship . . .

HALDER (*going to her, holding her*). Listen, you are not to leave me. You understand. Whatever it is. You and the kids. They're the whole basis of my life.

HELEN. Yes. I know . . . I know that, dear. I'll never leave you. You'll never leave me.

HALDER. I thought I'd tell you.

HELEN. I'm sorry . . . I'm tired, Johnnie . . .

HALDER. I'll come up soon . . . I'm waiting for this student . . .

HELEN. I love you.

HALDER. I love you. (*To the audience*:) I had to keep saying that to her. For *my* sake. Not to pacify her.

MAURICE. And the girl turned up with Richard Tauber?

HALDER. It's very complex. Unless you bear with me, Maurice and follow every strand . . . You won't get anywhere near the core of what is happening to me . . . If you will anyway . . . If there's anything to *get* to the core of, anyway . . .

She had an appointment with me that morning . . . So the tenor turning up in my office was clearly related to her coming to see me . . . *Could've* been Richard Tauber . . . He was singing 'You Are My Heart's Delight' . . .

The music comes up and the TENOR *appears on stage, singing.*

Yes . . . Probably *was* Tauber.

ANNE. *That's* what I find hard, Herr Doctor. Trying to find what it has to do with my life. Faust . . . or practically everything on the literature course . . . Goethe, especially, though . . . obviously he's Germany's greatest writer . . . There must be something missing in me.

HALDER. Tell me about your troubles in your lodgings.

ANNE. You see . . . It's ridiculous . . . I find what happens to me in my digs . . . I don't know why . . . profound . . . *important*, anyway . . . and what happens in Faust banal . . . trivial . . . How am I going to get a degree, with an attitude like that . . .

HALDER. That's what worries you, then.

ANNE. We're all in this flat in the Altstadt . . . I thought when I first went there . . . Wonderful, living in the old town . . .

HALDER. Next door to where Goethe was born.

ANNE. There's a dozen of us . . . And we're all alone. In this flat with Frau Stagl. She runs it for some capitalist.

HALDER. Jew.

ANNE. Probably . . .

Anyway, they're all so pathetic and interesting. There's a man

who has an obsession with trains . . . He plays them all night.
A couple of days ago one of the lodgers smuggled a woman
into his room. You should've seen her. At least forty-five . . . I
thought . . . Poor soul, you must be desperate . . .

HALDER. I can see that . . . Yes . . . Faust with his deep abstract
thoughts . . . In his study . . . Conjuring up rather tedious
depressing spirits spouting poetry . . . and the Devil with
his cheap conjuring tricks. And your fellow lodger with his
train set.

ANNE. Herr Doctor, what am I going to do? I'm never going to
get through my exams like this, am I?

HALDER. You didn't find my book on Goethe helpful?

ANNE. I found your two novels more *real* . . . I'm sorry . . . It's
just me . . .

HALDER. And this man who keeps knocking at your door?

ANNE. It's understandable. He gets confused. You see . . . there
are a couple of prostitutes in the house, too . . .

HALDER. Listen. I'd like to think about this. You've raised an
important point . . . The contemporary significance of Faust . . .
To your generation . . . Why don't we have another one to
one seminar . . . Very soon . . . This evening. Are you bush
this evening?

ANNE. Actually he's quite nice, this man who keeps knocking
at my door. Very tall. Lovely white teeth. It's just . . . He
gets on my nerves . . . Waking me up. I mean, he's not a
rapist or anything. He takes 'no' for an answer very calmly,
you know. 'Well, if you're not inclined . . . That's all right.
Pity. Sorry for troubling you.' I'm doing it again . . . I'm
sorry . . . Why am I coming out with all this rubbish, Herr
Doctor?

HALDER (*to himself*): She touched my hand! No. Our clothes
accidentally brushed together . . . My jacket and her
cardigan . . . That was all . . . I liked her in the matching
cardigan and jumper . . . I admit that . . .

ANNE. Yes . . . I'd like to come tonight. Very much. If you can spare the time, Doctor . . . That would be wonderful.

MOTHER. John . . . It's like a prison here. I want to get back to my own house.

HALDER. I'm organising everything, mother . . . There was a burst pipe . . . The whole house is damp, just now . . .

MOTHER. It doesn't matter . . . If there's food . . . As long as I can get back to my own bed.

HALDER. I've got the plumbers coming in . . .

MOTHER. Why can't I come to *you* for a week?

HALDER. You can come to me for a week. What happens *after* the week?

MOTHER. No . . . The best thing is to do away with myself . . . That'll be a finish to the whole problem.

HALDER (*checking his watch*). She's late.

MAURICE. Your mother turned up. This girl . . . And the band. You had a crowded evening.

HALDER. Richard Tauber came back for a final chorus, too . . . Maurice . . . Listen . . . What it could be . . . Is nothing I touch real? . . . Is it?

My whole life is like that . . . I do everything, more or less, that everybody else does . . . But I don't *feel* it's real. Like other people. On the other hand, it could be other people probably feel the same thing . . .

For Christ's sake, maybe I *am* in a bad way . . . So I'm entitled to pity myself a bit . . .

There's the door bell.

(*To the audience*): She was very pale and loveable. That was my first impression. Standing in the doorway . . . Wet . . . Her hair was dripping . . . And her coat . . . Soaked through. I'll put some more coal on the fire . . . Are you soaked through . . . Take my dressing-gown.

ANNE. I don't mind being wet.

HALDER. I'm going to give you a cognac . . . Will you take it?

ANNE. Yes, please . . . Thanks.

HALDER. Frau Halder's gone to bed. That doesn't mean you're late. She goes to bed early. One of her pleasures is reading in bed.

ANNE. Frau Stagl kept me back. She had an accident . . . Nothing much. She burned her arm . . . Cooking . . . I took her to hospital to get it dressed. She's fine now . . . but it took up all the evening . . . Waiting around.

HALDER. Would you like some smoked ham . . . and bread . . . I was going to have some, myself . . . Just before you came . . .

ANNE. Actually, I am hungry. Please . . . Shall I help you . . .

HALDER. I've got everything here . . .

(*To himself*:) That girl is definitely after me. Am *I* after her, that's the question . . . Could *be* . . .

(*To* ANNE:) Listen, you can't go all the way back to your digs tonight . . . It's still pouring . . . I'll bring you down some blankets . . . That couch is very comfortable . . . I've slept on it myself.

ANNE. Herr Doctor, I couldn't sleep *here*.

HALDER. And a pillow . . . We haven't got to the core of the problem yet, anyway.

ANNE. You see, I don't believe in evil. Not like Goethe seems to . . . Do you?

HALDER. That's what we have to talk about. It could be a way into Faust for you. While the examiners generally are looking for the same old stock answers to the stock questions . . . If a student does come up with a really original approach . . . Showing that he's taking a work they take so seriously as seriously himself . . .

(*To himself*:) She's *rousing* me.

Christ! She is! Where there's life, there's hope.

I've always thought there was a major flaw in me. Love . . . I never thought it was in me to love . . . To really love . . .

ANNE. If you get me the blankets . . . I'll make up the bed, Herr Doctor . . .

HALDER. Yes . . . I'll get them for you . . . Do you like two pillows or just one?

ANNE. I'd like two, please . . .

THE MAJOR, later known as FREDDIE (*coming to meet HALDER — outstretched hand*). Herr Doctor . . . Delighted to meet you . . . Please . . . Come in . . . You wish to join us . . . First class . . . Your father-in-law, Doctor Brunau telephoned me . . . He speaks so highly of you . . .

MAURICE. You joined the Nazis! *You* . . . For fuck's sake.

HALDER. I *told* you I joined the Nazis . . .

MAURICE. The reality is coming to me . . . Jesus . . . Johnnie . . . God in heaven . . .

HALDER. Facts of life . . .

He goes to ANNE.

Anne . . . I think I'd better tell you this. The last few months . . . You've been coming to me for seminars . . . What's happened is I've been getting emotionally attached to you . . .

ANNE. Have you? . . . Honestly?

HALDER. I don't know how it happened. I have.

ANNE (*going to him. Putting her arms round him. Kissing him passionately*). John . . . I love you . . . I can't believe it . . . I love you . . . I've loved you for months . . . And you love me me . . .

HALDER. I love you.

MAURICE. And you lost your erection?

HALDER. I was a bit overwhelmed by her response . . .

MAURICE. Panic?

HALDER. A bit . . . Yes . . .

Yes . . . I was frightened. In a panic. What was I letting myself

in for? I've got a first class job. Peace of mind. Wife . . .
kids . . .

And I'm suddenly jumping into the sea . . . I was bloody
terrified . . . The last person I wanted to see was Marlene
Dietrich . . . I never fancied her anyway . . .

Marlene Dietrich sings 'Falling in Love Again'.

I have a good wife . . . Reasonably attractive . . . Three
first-class children . . . A home . . . A growing reputation as a
critic and a novelist . . . I'm on the brink of committing
myself to the National Socialists and a completely new phase
of my life . . . To get myself involved in an affair with a
woman . . . You understand? . . .

What was I going to do? I had with a couple of sentences
unleashed the floodgates of a woman's heart as Goethe might
have said . . . Two women loved me . . . In these days, that was
a problem.

My God! My children! . . . What was going to become of
them . . . Where could I go? Where would we live? Anne
and I . . . In that sordid lodging house . . . It didn't even have
a proper garden . . . I needed a garden . . . And Helen . . . How
could I leave Helen . . .

You know how you get when you jump into the sea for the
first time like that . . . with a combination of guilt, brandy,
over-fatigue and general tension on top of ever present anxiety
neurosis . . .

I fell asleep. When I woke up, Helen was up, reading some
new book on keyboard technique . . .

HELEN. I woke up and couldn't get to sleep again. Did I wake
you?

HALDER. That student turned up, last night. Soaking wet. It
was pouring. So she's downstairs. In the lounge. I gave her
some blankets.

HELEN. That's all right. Will she be warm enough?

HALDER. I gave her some blankets.

Helen I want to talk to you. I've decided to join the Party. I had a long talk with your father. He's right. Basically . . .

HELEN. You told me that. Who's going to give her breakfast?

HALDER. *I'll* give her breakfast.

I didn't tell you about my decision.

HELEN. I *assumed*, in the end, you'd be sensible.

HALDER. I'm doing it because I love you . . . You know that. If it was just myself, I'd take a chance. I'm not one hundred per cent sure about Hitler . . . You understand that . . . I love you and the children . . .

HELEN. I know that.

HALDER. That's the whole foundation of my life.

HELEN. That's good.

HALDER. I'll never leave you.

HELEN. Why should you?

HALDER. You won't leave me?

HELEN. Why should I?

HALDER. Plenty of people leave each other.

HELEN. Plenty of people get knocked down by buses.

HALDER. That's a good observation.

HELEN. Well, they do. I'm glad. Father'll be glad, you joining the Party. It's a real commitment . . . You're not just joining to keep your job or get on in life . . .

HALDER. Am I not?

HELEN. You see . . . I don't do anything well . . . Do I? I'm useless . . .

HALDER. You're a good wife.

HELEN. I don't think I am.

HALDER. You are. You're the best wife in the world. I love you.

HELEN. *Do* you?

HALDER. You're my sweetheart, aren't you?

HELEN. Am I?

HALDER. You are. What are you?

HELEN. Your sweetheart . . .

BOULLER *enters with coffee.*

BOULLER. I brought the coffee in myself . . . To avoid
interruptions . . .

Halder, would it surprise you if I said Doctor Goebbels
himself had suggested your name to us? He drew our attention
to your novel . . . He was profoundly moved by it . . .
'Objectivity,' he said, 'combined with compassion and
humanity' . . .

HALDER (*to the audience*): They got me at a bad time. With my
mother in the state she got herself in . . . And the state I got
in at her state . . . I had to write all the guilt out in a pro
euthanasia novel . . .

BOULLER. You read the letter?

HALDER. You read the letter? (*Forgetting.*) I've read it. Yes . . .
Moving.

BOULLER (*taking up* HALDER's *novel*). The Leader himself
has looked over this. Do you know that? Would you like to
read his comment. (*Showing him.*) Look . . . In his own
writing . . .

HALDER (*to the audience*): God forgive me . . .

The human bloody being! The surge of pride in me! Reading
that scrawled sentence in Adolf's shaky hand — It said:
'Written from the heart!'

A Bavarian trio.

MAURICE. A Bavarian mountain *band*?

HALDER (*to the audience*): While Anne was in the bathroom
and the Bavarian Mountain Ensemble were singing their hearts
out, I kept moving from panic to romantic plans of going
back to nature with my beloved.

HALDER, *with the band, in songspiel.*

We'll go to Schwarzwald . . . Anne and I . . . Between Bernau and Wehr . . . There's a stretch of forest there, nobody goes into . . .

We'll build a rough hut. Dry. Warm. What do a man and a woman need to live? . . .

Now and then — I'll buy a rifle, of course — I'll shoot wild boar, deer . . .

HALDER *stops singing.*

It was irresponsible of me in my position to encourage her . . .

HALDER *starts again.*

A goat . . . We'll keep a goat . . . (*He falters and stops. The band falters, but then goes on*:) Can you keep a goat in the forest? Why shouldn't you? . . . I'm not talking about illegally living in the forest. Obviously, I'll have to buy some land . . . Four or five acres . . . I'd sell the house . . . Split the money two ways, between Helen and I . . . (*With sarcasm*:) I could gather folk tales from the natives and make a book out of them . . .

Everything under the pure sky . . . We eat, sleep, make love under the sun . . . or stars . . . whichever is about at the time of the activity . . .

(*With sarcasm*:) To the accompaniement of the Bavarian Mountain Ensemble . . .

The band stops.

I'm not sure if —

(*To* ANNE, *who wanders in wearing his dressing-gown*:) Are you musical? Do you play anything?

ANNE. I don't play anything. No. I like music but I never seem to be able to stand more than about the first movement of anything . . . I can sit through all the movements of Beethoven's Fifth . . . I don't mind that . . . Do you play? Obviously somebody does . . . with all that music around . . .

HALDER. No . . . I don't play. Look, will I take you into the university with me, this morning. Or do you want to go back to your lodgings first . . .

ANNE (*looking at him . . . drinking him in . . . in love*). I still
can't believe it! All the time I have been thinking 'He'll
never look at me'. And I've been in your mind . . . All the
time . . .

HALDER (*to* ANNE): You stood out, you see. . . As an
exceptional person . . . That is what drew me to you . . . You
are . . . There's no question about it . . . I'm drawn to you . . .
I like you very much . . . But you have to understand . . .

ANNE (*frightened now — waiting*). Yes . . . I want to understand.
I want to understand everything about you . . .

HALDER (*to* ANNE): When I said to you, last night, how much
I liked you . . . You might have got the wrong impression . . .
Sometimes I can be very inarticulate . . .

ANNE. Honestly . . . I feel it . . . You love me . . . Last night, I
felt it . . . This morning, you're fighting it . . . I know. It
must be frightening for you . . . I know that . . . Are you
frightened, love?

HALDER. I don't know where I am . . . No . . .

ANNE. Last night . . . You said you were emotionally involved
with me . . . You loved me . . .

HALDER (*to himself*): How could I not love you, my beautiful
darling . . .

You see . . . It's the children . . . I love them . . . I could never
leave my children . . . Being a father . . . you see . . .

ANNE. No. I can see that. You love them. They love you . . . I
suppose your wife being what she is . . . not being able to
cope . . . You have to be father and mother to them . . .

HALDER. They love their mother too . . .

ANNE. Do *you* love her, do you think? . . . Do you still love
her . . .

HALDER. Outsiders might think . . . with all the rubbish
littering the floors . . . My having to cook meals and send the
children to school . . . I don't say the pigsty here doesn't get

on my nerves at times . . . and not being able to invite people
to the house . . . without having a major cleaning operation . . .

ANNE. John . . . You're drowning . . . I'm not saying that because
I love you and I need you . . . You're drowning . . .

HELEN *comes in, in her dressing-gown.*

HELEN. I came down for more coffee. Is there any hot?
(*To* ANNE:) Has he fed you?

ANNE. Yes thank you. He made me eat a proper breakfast . . .

HELEN. I'm sorry the place is such a pigsty. I haven't been
coping with things.

ANNE. It's all right.

HELEN. Did you tell me her name, John?

ANNE. Anne.

You have lovely children . . . The girl's beautiful, isn't she?

HELEN. Did you make anything for me, John?

HALDER. I've fried you Liverwurst . . . I was just going to do an
egg for you.

HELEN. Were you warm enough here?

ANNE. It was wonderful. John had to wake me.

HELEN. You look very young. How old are you?

ANNE. I'm older than I look . . . I'm nearly twenty.

HELEN. I'm happy at thirty. I don't worry about not being young
any more. If I'm thirty. I'm thirty . . . I'm not *all* that bad
looking am I? What do *you* think?

A street musician, HITLER, *dressed in tweed plus-fours takes
up his stance, watched by* MAURICE *and* HALDER. *He plays
the first few bars of a Yiddish folksong.*

MAURICE. Jewish Wedding song. (*He sings:*) Came along Mrs
Bloom, brought along the handsome groom. Fine, fine,
Mrs Bloom, brought along the handsome groom.

. . . *Hitler?*

HALDER. I *think* it was Hitler. Might've been a bit of Charlie
Chaplin. I'm standing in the square by the fountain.
Paralysed. Not physically. Whatever part of me is responsible
for decision taking. That seemed to have gone out of
action . . . On my way to join the Party.

HITLER (*putting down his violin and addressing the world*).
Understandable. Totally understandable. You make a deal
with yourself one minute, you totally repudiate it the next.

(*To* MAURICE, *conversationally*:) Quite right. Absolutely
naive to think you can guarantee the minute you set yourself
on a course that you're going to hold it over the next sixty
seconds.

MAURICE. Sounds more like Chaplin than Adolf.

HITLER (*to the world*): The complexity of the human central
nervous system alone. All the forces playing on the human
organism . . .

MAURICE. Shit!

HITLER (*to the world*): Basically, what have we in a human
being? A complex electrical network. No. Even more complex
— a complex electrical and *chemical* network. (*To* MAURICE:)
Can you *get* chemical networks?

MAURICE. That's *conscious* shit.

You don't need the sub-conscious to handle scientific shit.
It deals with *real* shit.

HITLER (*to the world*): Man does not live by bread alone.

HALDER. I'm not sure about that.

HITLER (*conversationally*): I'm not sure about anything. That's
the human condition. 'Man you are born to uncertainty. You
can be sure of nothing.'

MAURICE. Sounds more like Chaplin than Adolf to me.

HITLER (*to the world*): For the first time in my life I am
breaking free from the emotional/physical umbilical cords
that tied me to my mother.

MAURICE. Now *that's* Hitler. *Pure, unadulterated* Hitler shit.

HITLER. Ring of the truth, but, Maurice.

MAURICE. Shit *has*.

HITLER (*to the world*): Breaking through to manhood. Completing myself as a human being . . . Establishing new emotional and physical umbilical strands with a woman I have chosen in my manhood. (*To* MAURICE:) Yes. I'm being pretentious and heavily profound. But it does happen. From time to time, you are confronted by profundities . . .

(*To himself:*) I have to get out of this . . . Apologising for any profound universal statement that comes to me.

MAURICE (*to* HALDER): You see . . . My fellow Jews. I can't stand them. My best friends are gentiles and Nazis.

HITLER (*to the world*): What is the objective reality? The objective reality is there is no objective reality. I don't know. *Who* knows?

How do I bring about a balance of the electrical and chemical forces in my body to make for something like the optimum functioning of myself as an organism?

HALDER. By joining the Nazis?

HITLER. But now I am moving to a soul union . . .

(*To* MAURICE:) What the fuck else is it, for Christ's sake? That's what it is. That's what I'm looking for. A soul union . . .

(*To the world:*) Now I am moving to a soul union.

Joining the Nazis is no longer a simple case of my own electrical and chemical state. It is *hers* too.

HALDER (*to* HITLER): That's what I'm telling you. I have to see Anne, first. Before I can make a definite decision.

HITLER (*to himself*): Yes. *Now* I understand *why* I have to see her.

HALDER. Do I?

MAURICE. This is a classic neurotic relationship. My best-loved friend is a Nazi!

HALDER. I had to talk to you about it first.

ANNE. You see . . . I'm not a political person. I wish I could help you more . . . I've never been able to get involved with politics . . . Just now . . . whatever you do would be all right to do . . .

HALDER. I couldn't make the move, you see . . . Till we talked about it . . .

ANNE. I'll try to help you . . . As much as I can . . . I hate them . . . being so down on the Jews . . . I hate that . . .

HALDER. Their ideal might be a Germany without Jews . . . But the *reality* is Jews are part of Germany . . . It's not real, a Germany without Jewish doctors, scientists, chemists . . . and *capitalists* for Christ's sake . . .

. . . Without Jewish capitalists . . .

ANNE. *I* think . . . you see . . . People just survive and live . . . It doesn't seem to matter what kind of government people have. They survived through all kinds of terrible times, didn't they?

You find somebody you love . . . and you have a family . . . and look after them . . . and try and not harm anybody . . . Isn't that what happens? . . . In the end you have to survive . . . And the less you harm people in surviving . . .

HALDER. It's not only survival, is it? Joining the Nazis. If people like us join them . . . instead of keeping away from them, being purist . . . And pushed them a bit towards humanity . . . Is that kidding yourself?

ANNE. What if they push *us* the other way?

HALDER. Yes . . . It could happen . . . Yes . . . If it did . . . I'd get out . . . No question about it . . . I'd pull myself away . . . I'd get out of the country . . . We'd get out of the country . . .

ANNE *is obviously thinking of something else*.

What are you thinking about, sweetheart?

ANNE. No . . . It's just . . . It's not good being frightened for yourself. When you're on your own. But being frightened for somebody you *love*.

HALDER (*arms round her*). We'll be all right. We'll help each
other, won't we? As long as we are together . . . I feel that.
That's the first time I've felt anything like that in my whole
life . . . It doesn't matter what happens round us . . . As
long as we have each other.

BOULLER (*with a letter*). Another letter we received only this
week on the same theme . . .

HALDER *taking the letter and reading it*.

The Chancellory is continually receiving requests from
relatives of people with incurable mental illnesses, for the
Leader's permission for mercy deaths for these patients . . .

This is, of course, just another aspect of the way Germans
are beginning to come to terms with the world and the human
situation as it *is* . . . Throwing away superstition and
mysticism and self-indulgent sentimentality.

HALDER. Which does not always lead to humanity and
compassion.

BOULLER. Halder, we want a paper from you. Arguing along the
same lines as you do in your novel, the necessity for such an
approach to mercy killings of the incurable and hopelessly
insane, on the grounds of humanity and compassion.

HALDER. The novel came out of a direct experience . . . My
mother's senile dementia.

BOULLER. Exactly. This is what makes your analysis so potent.
As the Leader says 'From the heart' . . . And I would add,
from the mind. I take it the opinions so clearly expressed in
your book, Halder, are firm personal convictions . . .

HALDER. Below a certain level of the quality of human life . . .
Yes . . . I can't see it worth preserving. From the individual
sufferer's point of view and his family's . . . Yes . . .

BOULLER. Look here, Professor . . . Let me be open and frank
with you . . . I could rest much easier in my bed, with your
participation in this project . . . You and I know how these
things can get out of hand . . . There are certain elements in
the party . . . And aside from that aspect . . . the inhumanities

that can happen in hospitals and other medical institutions.

. . . If we have you with us. You follow me? This would be for me, a guarantee that the whole question of humanity in the carrying out of this project would never be lost from the initial stages of planning, to the final implementation of the scheme.

HALDER. I'll draft out a paper for you, Over-Leader . . . In the next week . . .

BOULLER. That is *excellent*, Halder. First class . . . One copy only . . . And to be handed personally to me as soon as you have it . . .

A chorus of S.S. men . . . led by the MAJOR.

The MAJOR *goes forward to put his arm round* HALDER.

All with tankards of beer in their hands.

MAJOR (*singing to the tune of 'The Drinking Song' from the 'Student Prince'*):
> Drink, drink, drink,
> To eyes that are bright
> As stars when they're shining on me.
> Drink, drink, drink,
> To lips that are red and sweet
> As the fruit on the tree.
>
> Here's a hope
> That those bright eyes will shine,
> Lovingly, lovingly,
> Soon into mine.
> May those lips that are red and sweet,
> Tonight with joy my own lips meet.
> Drink, drink, let the toast start.
> May young hearts never part.
> Drink, drink, drink,
> Let every true lover salute his sweetheart.

HALDER (*to the audience*): It could have been the atmosphere of the place. The Nationalist Socialist Office was in this great house that belonged once to some great nobleman. Marble

Hall. Chandeliers . . . Turning everything into 'The Student Prince'.

. . . God forgive me! It was a wonderful feeling — joining. You have no idea, the emotional heights it lifted me to.

MAJOR. Listen, we're old comrades.

HALDER. Yes, I suppose we are.

MAJOR. You went into the Hessian Life Guards first. Remarkable.

HALDER. I'm not sure how I got in, you see . . . There was some confusion when I joined up in 1916 . . .

(*To the audience*:) It's a terrible thing. But it's a wonderful thing getting into a uniform. When I first got into my uniform in 1916 . . . All the emotions came back to me now . . . now . . . For the first week, Martin and I — a quasi-emotional homosexual relationship to be frank about it . . .

CHORUS (*sings*):
  Drink, drink etc.

HALDER. This friend I had. Martin . . .

MAJOR (*sings*):
  Here's a hope
  That those soft arms will twine etc.

HALDER (*to the audience*): We went around for the first week in uniform. Looking for officers to salute . . . One of the most exciting experiences in my youth. Walking around Stuttgart, saluting officers . . . Some of the swine didn't even look at us . . . Turned their heads in the opposite direction . . .

. . . And now joining the Party . . . Not just joining. But being taken in like a brother.

MAJOR. Herr Doctor . . . You can't just join the S.A. How can a man like you, join the S.A.? That amuses me. The modest opinion you have of yourself.

HALDER. I hadn't . . . I'll be honest with you, Major . . . I hadn't heard of the S.S.

MAJOR. The S.S., you see, Doctor . . .

CHORUS (*sings*):
    Drink, drink etc.

MAJOR. Let me tell you something. I never tell this to the
    usual applicants . . . You understand? But look here . . . John
    Halder . . . The Goethe man . . . My wife is a great reader . . .
    I'm sure she must have read several of your books . . . And
    your father . . . *The Roman Man* . . .

    Now . . . That book, I read . . . Obviously such a deep book
    as that, I just got the gist of it, but that wonderful discovery
    he made . . . 'The true and pure German culture can be
    found only in that part of Germany the Romans failed to
    contaminate' . . . You see, I still remember bits of it . . .

    Look here, I'm going to lunch shortly. Lunch with me . . .
    Please . . . I want to talk to you in detail about the S.S.

CHORUS (*sings*):
    Drink, drink etc.

HALDER (*to the audience*): They loved me. You see? I was an
    old soldier . . . and the Goethe Man . . . If they love you like
    that, you can't help loving them back. Freddie, the Major,
    gave me smoked ham and baked potatoes and Frankfurt
    Cyder . . .

MAJOR. Better than wine, eh? Our Apfelwein . . .

    . . . The Kaiser had his own elite regiment . . . , as you know,
    The Imperial Guard, and, of course, now we have our elite. The
    S.S. Clearly, that is the only place for you. In the elite along
    with us.

HALDER (*to the audience*): He was such a nice, open man . . .
    His father was a school teacher . . . So was his wife's
    father . . . He wasn't a cliché Nazi ex-jailbird thug . . . And
    he told me what Hitler had said to him . . .

MAJOR. I can hear his voice, now. That Austrian accent. Pleasant,
    quiet, concerned. He was so concerned about us.

HALDER. }   I should like to make you two pledges. I will
HITLER.   }   never give a command to march against the lawful
    government of Germany — that is, I will never attempt a

second time to come to power by force.

MAJOR. We all looked at him. Everybody was surprised. This is
1932 I am talking about. The terrible conditions. Inflation.
Unemployment. Children in the streets in winter without
shoes . . .

HALDER. ⎫   And I promise you, I will never give you an order
HITLER ⎬   which goes against your conscience.

MAJOR. 'I will never give you an order which goes against your
conscience' . . . And the way he said it, you see . . .

CHORUS (sings).
    Drink, drink etc.

Act Two

MAURICE (*grabbing* HALDER). Listen to me, Nazi cunt! I'm fucking talking to you! You hear me?

HALDER. Maurice, I'm *listening*.

MAURICE. For fuck's sake! This *obscenity*, Johnnie. I never use obscene language like this . . . I don't *need* to use obscene language . . .

HALDER (*to himself*): I don't mind the obscenities and the abuse. It's understandable. But I want to get down to business and go home. The whole situation is throwing me into panic. Coming here, to a *Jewish house*. That's a highly dangerous action, for God's sake!

MAURICE. What was I saying to you, Johnnie? I got so lost in abuse and obscenities, I've forgotten what I was saying to you.

HALDER (*to himself*): The whole situation depresses me. That was one of the highlights of my week. A quiet, relaxing evening of communication with my one friend over a Jewish dinner . . . completely *destroyed!* I can't even *speak* to him on the telephone now, without being thrown into panic . . .
(*To* MAURICE:) You're my *one bloody friend*. You know that . . . (*To himself*:) And he's got to be *Jewish!*

MAURICE. Get me these exit papers, then, Nazi cunt! Fucking *do* something about this *fucking great friendship,* then for fuck's sake!

Jesus! What am I *doing?* Listen, Johnnie . . . Don't pay any attention to it . . . This is just my filthy unconscious coming to the surface . . . My whole defences have totally collapsed . . . It's nothing to do with my real feelings for you . . . I love you . . .

I *do* . . . Jesus . . . I do . . .

HALDER. You know that, Maurice . . . How can I get you exit
papers? If I could, I would . . . You know that . . .
(*To himself*:) I love him. No question about it. I love him.
But I am not going to prison for him. I couldn't stand going
to a Nazi prison. (*To* MAURICE:) I'm looking at this meal
we're sitting down to.

MAURICE. You're a fucking Nazi S.S. officer, for fuck's sake.
You can find some way of getting me out of this fucking
country! For fuck's sake! Listen to the fucking language
pouring out of me!

HALDER. Maurice, this is a circular discussion, leading
nowhere . . . You know that . . .

MAURICE. Come with me, Johnnie. If you came with me, I
could *stand* leaving Germany. That would make it bearable.
If we were together. Listen. I know . . . Both of us . . . We
don't take to all that many people . . . What kind of life would
it be here, without me?

HALDER. You're in an anxiety state, Maurice . . . You know
that . . . Engulfed in a 'subconscious storm'. Your own
words . . .

MAURICE. I'm *lost,* Johnnie . . . *Totally, utterly lost* . . . Do
you know what's happening to me?

HALDER. Look at this meal, Maurice. We sit down to a meal
that would cost a worker, if he's lucky, what he earns in a
week . . . That's the *real* issue, just now.

MAURICE. *More*! The wine alone is a week's wages.

HALDER. We can't go on like this, can we? . . . You as a
Socialist . . . Me as a Socialist . . . How long can you go on
crying about the poverty of the workers while you are living
off the fat of the land . . .

MAURICE. Johnnie . . . Johnnie . . . This is my fucking home . . .
I'm like in mourning . . . I'm bereaved . . . You know that? . . .
The idea of being cut off for the rest of my life from my
place in Burgsinn. I've put up nesting boxes for the spring . . .

I went out and bought special nesting boxes . . . For woodpeckers . . . We were looking forward to woodpeckers nesting at the back of our cottage . . .

HALDER (*to himself*): I want to talk to him about that cottage. (*To* MAURICE:) I want to talk to you about the cottage.

MAURICE. I come *alive* there. The trees . . . And the green . . . I was bloody *born* here . . . My father was *born* here . . . My grandfather . . . Listen . . . I don't even *like* Jews . . . I like my wife and kids . . . But generally . . .

HALDER. I don't like *anybody* all that much . . .

MAURICE. That's true . . .

Listen Johnnie, for Christ's sake . . . You've got to help me get out of here . . . Are you listening to me . . .? You've got to *help* me! We've both got to get out of here!

MOTHER (*trapped in a corner — lost — frightened*). John . . . John . . . John . . . For God's sake . . . Where am I?

HALDER (*rushing to her*). Where do you think you are, mother?

MOTHER. It's no use. Take me back to the hospital . . . I'll never manage to live here on my own. Take me back . . . I'm collapsing . . .

HALDER. Just try, mother . . . Try to get a picture of your house in your mind . . .

MOTHER. Am I in the kitchen?

HALDER. No. You're in the bedroom.

MOTHER. I'm in the bedroom? (*Groping about her.*) It's no use, son, I'm finished. I can't take it in . . . I'll go back to the hospital.

HALDER. I'll take you over to the bed again. (*Leading her.*) Try to picture it in your mind . . . Your room. Put your hand on the bed.

MOTHER. It's no use, I tell you I'm finished.

You have got your own life to lead. Go back to Frankfurt, son. I'll go into some institution.

HALDER. Follow the edge of the bed, mother . . . hand . . . Think . . .

MOTHER. I can't think. It's all going from my brain.

HALDER. Think of the room . . . You remember the room before you lost your . . .

MOTHER. It's all going out of my brain, I'm telling you I can't . . . (*Desperately trying.*) This is the bedroom wall? (*Feeling.*) That's the bed cabinet . . .

HALDER. Try again, mother . . . Work out what it is . . . How can that be the cabinet?

MOTHER (*feeling*). It's the table.

HALDER. That's right.

MOTHER. And that's the way to the door?

HALDER (*giving up — despairing*). That's the window.

A burst of flames at the rear of the stage. A bonfire is in progress.

Jazz trio playing jazz 'Hold That Tiger'.

BOK, *carrying a load of books, turns to* HALDER.

BOK. What about these? They're in French. Can't make them out.

HALDER (*looking at the titles*). 'Recherche du Temps Perdu . . .'

BOK. Eh?

HALDER. Remembering the past.

BOK. Oh, well . . . They might as well go too. Don't want to waste any time on the past, do we? . . . Here you are, lads . . . (*He throws the books on the bonfire.*) Fancy French dish in for you bonfire.

S.S. MAJOR, *now known as* FREDDIE, *bottle in his hand, calls to* HALDER.

FREDDIE. Brandy, Johnnie?

HALDER (*going to him*). Good party. Freddie. We're both enjoying ourselves . . . (*As he is talking,* ANNE *approaches with* ELISABETH, FREDDIE's *wife.*)

ELISABETH. Freddie, I want to talk to you for a minute. John, why didn't you *tell* us about your accommodation problem?

(*To* FREDDIE:) These two poor children have nowhere to live.

ANNE. We'll find somewhere. It's just that John has to live somewhere where there are fields and open spaces.

FREDDIE. I'm just going to have a quick word with Johnnie, Liz, my love.

ELISABETH. We're going to choose our May Queen. Where are you going?

FREDDIE. Choose Anne. Look at her! Why can't *I* have women like that falling for me.

ELISABETH. Freddie, they need somewhere to live . . . Desperately.

FREDDIE. We'll organise that. Don't worry about it.

ELISABETH. We will be choosing the May Queen and the May King at nine precisely.

FREDDIE. I just want a minute with him, Liz . . .

HALDER (*turning to the* DOCTOR). What a pleasant place this is, Doctor.

DOCTOR. It hasn't been a private residence for many years.

HALDER. All the courtyards and archways.

DOCTOR. It was sold for an orphanage. Then it became a hospital, Herr Professor.

. . . Your field is *literature* then? . . . I see . . .

HALDER. I think Berlin sees me as some kind of humanity expert . . . My role is to look round, assess the arrangements and make some recommendations on general humane grounds.

DOCTOR. Yes . . . I understand . . . I see . . . We had thought, of course, you were a medical man . . . What would you like to do first? Meet the staff?

HALDER. I think I'll just wander around, if you don't mind . . .

DOCTOR. I'll get someone to show you round. That's the best thing . . . One of our medical staff, I think . . . He can explain the medical ins and outs.

Fats Waller: 'My Very Good Friend the Milkman'.

FREDDIE (*opening a case*). I'm going to let you into this, to show I trust you, Johnnie . . . Both of us . . . Our records . . . We don't need to goosestep round the square, shouting 'Heil Hitler' to prove we're good Party people.

. . . Look here, there's an order come through for you. I'd rather we didn't make it an order . . . You know that . . . This particular order especially . . . Because I can understand how you'll feel about it . . . (*Opening a box.*) We all have our vices . . . Our private secrets . . .

. . . Not a man hasn't something he doesn't want anybody else to know about. . .

HALDER. If it's an order — give it to me. It's all right, Freddie . . .

FREDDIE. I'm letting you into my vice. Records. (*Drawing out a file . . . opening it . . .*)

HALDER. Gramophone records . . . (*Clearly disappointed.*)

FREDDIE. That's it.

HALDER. Military marches . . .

FREDDIE. That's what it says on the labels . . . See . . .

HALDER. Jazz . . .

FREDDIE. I changed all the labels. Took me weeks . . . You know the Party line on decadent negroid swamp jungle music. Opium . . .

. . . I'll tell you something . . . I know this for a fact. The Great Man . . . Up in Berlin . . . You know his favourite film . . . ? Jew Charlie Chaplin . . . Watching Charlie Chaplin till midnight . . . every night.

. . . I can't help it. I've been playing Jazz since I was called up . . . Used to have a sergeant in my squad . . . Got killed in Verdun . . . He played the fiddle . . . He played the blues . . . Soothed me . . .

HALDER. I'm trying to listen to the music.

FREDDIE. . . . Soothes me that music . . . Christ knows you need

soothing in this bastard job at times. Building up a country
from fuck all. What did those Social Democrat shits leave us?
A fucking shit heap . . . I'm sorry . . . I don't usually talk
like that . . . But it's true.

HALDER. It's a nice tune . . . (*To himself*:) What else can you say?

FREDDIE. I haven't any *real* friends . . . I haven't . . . Have you?
. . . Apart from your woman, I mean.

. . . Between you and me . . . Most of the comrades . . . They're
good lads . . . But they piss me off, after an hour or so . . :
Only one who doesn't seem to piss me off's you. Probably
because you're educated . . . I don't know . . . At times, *you*
piss me off, too, of course . . .

HALDER. Mutual.

FREDDIE. I know I piss you off . . . No question about that . . .
(*He hands him a paper*.) That's the list.

HALDER (*studying it*). Oh . . . I like him . . . I like everybody . . .
It's just *books*. It's a list of books.

(*Reading*:) I see . . . I'm ordered to organise the Book Burning
Ceremony at the university.

FREDDIE. When it came through you see . . . I said to myself:
'Johnnie's got deep feeling about books . . . This is going to
cut him deeply I can see that.'

HALDER. Long list . . . Thomas Mann . . . Remarque . . .

FREDDIE. I read that. *All Quiet on the Western Front*. Don't
ask me why they've done a downer on that. That's exactly how
it was at the front, wasn't it?

HALDER (*to himself*): There's a positive aspect to all this.
You've got to make a supreme effort and look positively . . .
One of the basic defects of university life is learning from
books. Not from *experience* . . . Life . . . *involvement* . . .
commitment . . . agony and panic at being thrown into the
storm that's the human condition . . .

FREDDIE. Mind, I can see what they're getting at, burning Freud's
filthy shit. Pervert, isn't he? Tried to make out everybody's
as twisted and perverted as he is!

HALDER (*to himself*): If you looked at it from the philosophical standpoint, that the burning is symbolic of a new healthy approach to university learning . . . Man does not live by books alone.

FREDDIE. All right, Johnnie? Can I leave that to you?

HALDER. As long as I can keep *my* copies, Freddie.

FREDDIE. *I've* got my jungle music, haven't I?

Lieder SINGER *in evening dress.*

HELEN *at the keyboard.*

Schubert's 'Ständchen' . . .

SINGER.
> Gently floating, through the evening,
> Hear this song for you.
> In this quiet,
> Grove below you,
> Waits your lover true.

HALDER (*to the audience*): You might think what a bloody ridiculous thing to be doing, writing out a recipe for goulash for your wife who you are about to leave. But if you think about it, it's sensible enough, if she can't *cook* . . . Anyway, it was something practical to do, while she was practising Schubert . . .

(*To* HELEN:) It's a simple recipe, Helen. You see . . . I've written it out in simple stages . . .

HELEN. John, you're so pale. You don't look well.

HALDER (*to himself*): That's a good approach. Excellent. Go on, make it really difficult. Be understanding.

I am very sorry for that woman. All my compassion goes out to her. I'm failing her . . . I'm failing *myself* even worse.

HELEN. Are you just going to leave me one *recipe* before you run off to the forest with her?

HALDER. Helen, I don't know what I'm doing. (*To himself:*) Who says I'm running off?

(*To* HELEN:) I don't know if I'm going anywhere . . . I'm
just writing this recipe . . . Because it's easy . . . All you need
is a tin of meat . . .

HELEN. It looks easy enough on paper, but I'm not sure there's
not something wrong with me. I don't seem to be able to
co-ordinate things . . . I get obsessed with the wrong order.
When I make a stew I get obsessed with the potatoes to be
cooked and cook them . . . before the meat . . .

HALDER. I don't know *what* I'm going to do . . .

HELEN. I hate it when you suffer like this . . . Look at you.

HALDER. Why have you turned so bloody understanding all
of a sudden?

HELEN. I don't know . . . Have I? . . . I'm just lost . . . That's
all . . . The worst thing . . . You know what the worst thing
is . . .

MOTHER (*shouting*). John! John . . . Helen . . .

HALDER. I'll be up in a minute, mother . . .

MOTHER. I need to go to the toilet.

HALDER. What was the worst thing . . .

MOTHER. John!

HALDER. You've just *been* to the bloody toilet!

MOTHER. I need to go again. Have I got to have set hours when
I go and don't go . . .

HELEN. *I'll* take her.

HALDER. She's *my* mother . . . You take her all day . . . Stop
being so nice to me will you . . .

. . . I'm coming . . .

I'm here, mother . . .

MOTHER. I'm very sorry. I can't get my bowels to make a
timetable for me, son,

. . . Where's the seat?

HALDER (*guiding her*). There you are . . . I'll wait outside for you.

MOTHER. Wait outside . . . Stay inside . . . What difference does it make to me now . . .

HALDER. I'll wait outside . . .

MOTHER. John . . . What's going to happen to me if you run off with that prostitute from Altstadt? . . . Don't kid yourself, she's in love with you . . . She knows when she's got a mug . . . With a position and a good income . . .

. . . Where the toilet paper?

. . . My God. I can't find it. This miserable house . . . They don't even have any toilet paper . . . I knew it was an unlucky house the first time I stepped through the door . . .

HALDER. There's the toilet paper, for God's sake.

Mother . . . Why the hell did you have to tell Helen about Anne?

MOTHER. Where's the wash-hand basin? I need to wash my hands . . .

HALDER. Follow the wall . . . Use your imagination . . . You'll never be able to bloody live on your own if you don't give yourself a shake . . .

MOTHER. I'm sorry, son . . . I can't perform for you . . . I can't take it in . . . and be independent, so you can run off with your prostitute and leave me on my own without feeling guilty . . .

. . . Where's the bloody tap . . .

HALDER. Use your imagination . . .

MOTHER. I can't wash my hands with imagination, son. Maybe you can.

God in heaven . . . The women you pick . . . I told you from the beginning . . . Your father did . . . That woman is no good to you . . . Didn't we plead with you . . . The night before your wedding. To call it off . . .

. . . Where are you taking me now?

HALDER. I'm taking you back to the bedroom.

MOTHER. I've been stuck up there all day. I want to go downstairs . . . What are you going to do about the children?

HALDER. They'll be all right . . . I'll look after them.

MOTHER. That woman. Dear God, she can't even make a cup of coffee. She gave me bread and butter this morning . . . The bread was cut like doorsteps . . . I want to go *downstairs* . . .

HALDER. Sit in your room a minute . . .

MOTHER. Will you take me downstairs . . . What do you think you're doing . . . Torturing me here . . . Locking me up like a prisoner with not a soul coming to see me all day . . . If that is what you wanted to do . . . Giving me a holiday with you . . . You should never have taken me out of the hospital . . .

HALDER. I'll come back in a minute . . . *I* need to go to the toilet . . .

(*To the audience*): Helen was in the kitchen. Trying to cook the recipe I'd written out for her.

(*To himself — watching her*:) It could well be there is a vestigial brain damage. Not all that much. A trace. That stops her cooking and cleaning the house. And, of course, relating to me as deeply and fully as I need.

HELEN. You *fry* the onions first?

HALDER. You don't need to do it this *minute*, do you?

HELEN. I'm doing it now. While you're here to put me right.

Up till a few months ago . . . I wouldn't have felt it so much . . . You saying you love somebody else . . . Now when you say it . . . It's like a cold hand reaching into my intestines . . .

. . . I loved you a bit during our honeymoon . . . and after . . . Then just a few months ago . . . I really started falling in love with you . . . It surprised me . . . I don't know why . . . Did you notice?

HALDER. Yes . . . (*To the audience*:) Well when your wife suddenly comes out with something like that for Christ's sake.

(*To* HELEN:) I think so . . .

HELEN. Probably my instinct told me I was losing you . . . So I began to realise what I was losing . . . *I* don't know . . .

HALDER (*to himself*): She's not frying the *meat*.

(*To* HELEN:) You have to fry the meat too, Helen.

HELEN. That's right . . .

The idea of losing you . . .

HALDER. You're *not* losing me.

HELEN. Just . . . My whole life really . . . It's round you . . . That's the basis of my whole life . . .

HALDER (*to himself*): You're not losing me . . . I'll never leave you . . .

(*To* HELEN:) I won't leave you.

(*To himself*:) What do I mean by that . . . I won't . . .

HELEN. Don't just say things to pacify me, John . . . will you not, love? . . . I couldn't stand that . . .

MOTHER. John . . . John . . .

HALDER. Oh, Jesus . . . I cannot cope with that bloody woman just now . . .

MOTHER. John . . .

HALDER. I'm coming . . .

MOTHER. I thought you were in the toilet.

HELEN. What are you going to do with her . . . If you have any ideas, tell me . . .

MOTHER. John . . .

HALDER (*going*). I'm coming.

HELEN. I don't understand you, John. What do you mean . . . you're not leaving me . . . ?

HALDER. I don't know . . .

(*To himself*:) What do I mean?

(*To* HELEN:) I'll be in every day to see you and the children . . . Make sure you're all right.

HELEN. If you're living miles away . . . In the forest . . .

HALDER. I've got to come into the university . . . I have
    Storm Meetings . . . All kinds of things to do in Frankfurt . . .

HELEN (*indicating the food*). Is this right?

HALDER. That's fine.

MOTHER. John . . . John . . .

HELEN. I wish I could help you . . . I do . . . It's a shame for
    you . . . I know . . . It's me . . .

HALDER. I'd better get that bloody woman downstairs . . .

HELEN. I haven't any *friends* . . . I could never make friends . . .
    Never at any time . . . I never had any real friends . . . Except
    you . . .

MOTHER. John . . .

HALDER. I'm bloody coming!

    (*To* HELEN:) You still have me . . . As your friend . . .

HELEN. When I started loving you . . . The children irritated
    me . . . Their continual bloody presence . . . I just wanted the
    two of us to be on our own . . . Just stupid fantasies . . . You
    know what I'm like . . .

MOTHER. John . . . John . . .

HALDER. I'll bring you down in a bloody minute!

MOTHER. I don't *want* to go down. I need to go to the *toilet!*

    A DOCTOR *wheels in a severely mentally handicapped woman.*

DOCTOR. You have to ask yourself, as you did in your novel . . .
    Which moved me deeply, Herr Professor . . . When you come
    to this level . . . Is this *human* life? She has no control over her
    bladder or bowels . . . The dimmest awareness of her
    environment and what is happening round her . . .

HALDER. We can take the arguments as read I think, Doctor.
    What we have to make sure of is that the procedure is carried
    out humanely . . . Their last hour must be absolutely free from
    any trace of anxiety . . .

DOCTOR. Absolutely . . . Of course . . .

HALDER. This room is adequate . . . But it needs to be much
more ordinary and reassuring . . . Could it be made to look
like a bathroom, perhaps . . . So that the patients are
reassured and believe they are being taken for a bath . . .

DOCTOR. Yes. So they come in here . . . Ostensibly for a bath . . .
A normal daily routine . . .

HALDER. What about the families? This is very important . . .
Exactly how the families are informed will have to be
carefully worked out . . . In detail . . .

DOCTOR. Of course, Herr Professor . . . Of course, they'll be
bound to accept the doctor's word on the death certificate . . .

HALDER. I'd like a meeting of everybody concerned, after
lunch, Doctor, to discuss this in detail . . . The families have
had enough pain as it is, looking *after* poor souls like her . . .

Music: 'Carolina in the Morning'.

MAURICE (*shivering*). What are we *doing* here? Sitting in the
middle of a cold, freezing, miserable fucking park in the
middle of winter!

HALDER (*following the band*). The interesting thing, Maurice,
is I am not consciously aware I ever knew that song.
'Carolina in the Morning'.

MAURICE. I don't know it . . . It's like lovers. Having secret
meetings . . . In any case, I don't think it's a good idea. It's
suspicious, coming here. Who goes to *parks* in the middle of
winter!

HALDER. No. I've established that as a regular routine. Every
day about this time, I go for a walk in the park.

MAURICE. I'm *freezing,* for God's sake!

HALDER. You should've brought a warm sweater, Maurice.
(*To himself:*) This friendship. All I get from it now, is pain,
anxiety and panic. I *know*. This is not *good*. The shallowness
of my feelings for the one friend I have in the world. (*Looking
at* MAURICE.) On the other hand. I could be underestimating

my love for him. My feelings may not be quite as shallow as I imagine. I *have* gone out of my way to meet him here, just now . . . I know. I'm after his cottage . . . But it's not entirely that . . . Is it? . . . (*To* Maurice:) Going to your house, Maurice. During this temporary racialist aberration. It's not a sensible action . . . For your sake or mine.

MAURICE. So how does the cat come over the water? *I* can't come to *your* house.

HALDER. *Worse*. Coming to *my* house.

MAURICE. Listen, Johnnie . . . I know . . . I can understand that . . . You can't get me these exit papers . . . I know . . . It's asking too much of you . . .

HALDER (*to himself*): What is coming clear to me, now . . . I had thrown away the concept of cowardice and courage. I can see now. There is some meaning to them. To some extent, there is an element of cowardice in my failing Maurice like this . . . At the same time, All these people depending on me. (*To* MAURICE:) If it was just myself. But I have two wives, two children and a blind mother, Maurice . . .

MAURICE (*handing him a parcel*). I brought you some cheesecake . . . Where will you get Jewish cheesecake, when you've locked up all the Jews?

HALDER (*alarmed*). Is that somebody coming? Somebody's coming. Feed the pigeons, Maurice.

MAURICE. Nobody's coming . . .

HALDER. Feed the pigeons, Maurice . . .

MAURICE. I've nothing to feed the fucking pigeons with!

HALDER (*offering the cheesecake*). Here. Give them some cheesecake.

MAURICE. I'm not feeding good, Jewish *cheesecake* to fucking *pigeons!*

HALDER. There is somebody coming.

MAURICE. They've come to listen to your band. It's an unusual attraction for the park in winter.

HALDER. It's all right. They've gone down the other path . . .
Maurice . . . I don't want to push you about the cottage . . .
But if we could have it even just for a few months .'. . You're
not using it anyway, just now . . . It would be exactly the
right start for us . . . Somewhere like your cottage . . .

MAURICE. Walking through the forest, hand in hand, with the
love of your life . . . At dawn . . . The way the sun comes
through the trees at dawn sometimes. The shafts of
sunlight . . . Yes. It's a beautiful picture. It lifts the whole
sexual element right up . . . You're right. It's a beautiful
picture.

HALDER (*to himself*): Yes. That was a superficial evaluation
of my feelings for him. I still love him. Just for the moment,
love has been obscured by panic and anxiety . . .

MAURICE. You understand what I'm saying, Johnnie . . . It's
too much to ask from you. The exit papers . . . Forget the
papers . . . Just get me five tickets to Switzerland . . .

HALDER. Maurice . . . how can I go to the station and ask for
five single tickets to Switzerland, for God's sake!

MAURICE. Ask for *returns*.

HALDER. Or returns. I'm a bloody officer in the S.S.

MAURICE. That cheesecake. I bought it at Epstein's. I can't
stand them. I can't stand *Jews*. I spent thirty-five Marks in
there at one go, and they couldn't even give me a 'good
afternoon' . . . You're right. There's something seriously
wrong with Jews. I can see Hitler's point.

HALDER. With people.

MAURICE. That's what I said. With people . . . I'm talking about
what kind of fucking neurotic am I? *Jews*, in the same boat
as me, who have done me no wrong except they don't wish
me a 'good afternoon', I can't stand. Nazis, who want to
crucify me, I buy cheesecake for!

HALDER. Another word for a human being, Maurice.
'Neurotic . . .'

MAURICE. Listen. A major insight like that! We should send a telegram to Freud! . . . Johnnie . . . Take the cottage. Use it in health and joy. I won't need it in Switzerland.

HALDER. You don't need to go anywhere, Maurice. I don't want you to go anywhere . . . This is a temporary racialist aberration. Hitler's not going to survive another six months. You said that yourself . . .

This is still a capitalist country. The real power is in the hand of the capitalists . . . They can't afford to have a mystic idealist running their country . . . You know that . . . This is a temporary aberration . . .

MAURICE. It's a basic biological drive, you see, Johnnie . . . When people come after you with fucking machine guns, you start running . . . Look at me . . . I'm calm. I am looking at this cold and rationally . . . Yes . . . It's a temporary aberration . . . The trouble is, with all the machine guns in this fucking country, it's not going to take all that long a temporary aberration to finish off the whole Jewish population . . .

HALDER (to himself): I love Jews. I'm attracted to their whole culture. Their existence is a joy to me. Why have they got to be a bloody problem to everybody? (To MAURICE:) You know that, Maurice . . . Nobody takes that metaphysical racialist rubbish in *Mein Kampf* seriously . . . Pure races and foul, perverted, spiritually-riddled-with-disease Jews . . . Nobody can even *read* it!

MAURICE. He doesn't listen to people. I'm telling you. There is legislation coming in the next few days . . . In the next day. Today . . . Maybe *yesterday*. Against men without foreskins . . . I *know* that . . . Laws . . . I've got fucking hard information. *Now,* will you get me five tickets to Switzerland? No, you won't . . . You don't give a shit what happens to me . . . Understandable . . . (*Turning to go*.) Listen. It's cold. I've enough on my head without getting pneumonia . . .

HALDER. When you're out of your anxiety state, Maurice, you'll see that for yourself . . . Hitler is not going to survive . . . They got rid of Röhm and they'll get rid of Hitler . . . It's going to be all right.

MAURICE. Yes. For you, it'll be beautiful. For Nazi cunts it's going to be a beautiful, golden world.

HALDER. We'll talk about it, when you're calmer, Maurice . . .

MAURICE. Yes. When I'm lying on the ground, riddled with fucking Nazi cunt machine-gun bullets.

HALDER (*to the audience*): . . . *He* was cutting himself off from *me*. Good. I was free from him. Then he turned back and looked at me. No, I said to myself, watching him: 'I didn't think it would be as easy a parting as that.'

MAURICE. Listen. You'll have to run from here. For your fucking life, Johnnie. As much as me . . . Maybe even more than me . . .

DOCTOR. If you come in here, Herr Professor . . . You can meet some of the patients . . .

HALDER. What is vital, Doctor, is to look fully into their families . . . The quality or lack of quality of their relationships to the patients . . . How often they visit them . . .

DOCTOR. Absolutely, of course . . .

HALDER. I'd like to talk to some of the relatives . . .

DOCTOR. One or two, Herr Professor, have expressed strong views about the pointlessness of the existence of human parodies like these . . . I am using their words, of course . . .

HALDER (*to a patient*): Hullo . . . Is that your doll? (*No response.*) What do you call it? . . . Does he behave himself? (*To the* DOCTOR:) I'd suggest something like the families being told the patients are being sent here for a new course of treatment . . .

DOCTOR. Or perhaps a routine transfer . . .

HALDER. The patients should not have the slightest grounds for alarm or anxiety . . .

DOCTOR. We are planning to hold to the normal procedures, Herr Professor . . . On arrival, each patient would be examined by a doctor . . . A thorough examination . . .

HALDER. And no delay . . . It would be intolerable if they

stayed here any length of time . . .

DOCTOR. Absolutely, Herr Professor . . . Once the decision has been reached to terminate . . .

Up bonfire.

The CHANCELLOR touches the bonfire with his torch . . . a mass of flames . . .

Music: Wagner.

ANNE. What is in your mind, John? That is the most important thing, the beliefs in your mind . . . I don't know . . .

HALDER. It's political hysteria for the minute . . . Hitler being in power . . . Getting drunk with success . . . Once the hysteria's over . . . I told Maurice this . . .

ANNE. Do you *think* it is?

HALDER. What about Freddie's summer house by the river?

ANNE. Liz is taking me tomorrow to look at it . . .

HALDER. It was a nice party . . . It was nice . . . When they crowned you May Queen . . . I know it's stupid . . . But I had this feeling of pride . . .

ANNE. I looked as though I'd stepped out of 'The Rheingold' in that dress.

HALDER. You're lovely.

ANNE. I love you and you love me.

HALDER. I do . . . But . . .

The bonfire flares up.

ANNE. I don't know what it is . . . These books . . . When I think about them burning the books . . . I just say to myself: 'It's just a gesture. It doesn't mean anything. Most people. They're not even aware they exist.' I'm frightened.

HALDER. I know . . . You're right. That's exactly the feeling . . .

ANNE. Do you have it?

HALDER. I went into a fever hospital when I was four . . . Scarlet fever . . . They came for me during the night . . . A nurse carried me away from my room . . .

ANNE *throws her arms round* HALDER. *They cling to each other.*

ANNE. All we can do is hold on to each other. If we're good to each other. And the people round us . . . If we try to the utmost to be good . . .

The bonfire flares up.

What else can we do?

HALDER. I haven't even read Einstein.

Up bonfire. The Bach fugue.

CROONER.
Day is ending. Birds are wending.
Back to the shelter of
Each little nest they love.
Nightshades falling.
Lovebirds calling.
What makes the world go round.
Nothing but love.

FREDDIE *carries in a load of freshly cut logs.* ELISABETH *is dancing.*

FREDDIE. Two things I enjoy. I love polishing boots till you can see your face in them . . . And making fires . . . I'm a born hotel porter, aren't I?

CROONER.
When whipper wills call,
And evening is nigh,
I hurry to my
Blue heaven.
A turn to the right,
A little white light,
Will lead you to my
Blue heaven.

ELISABETH. It's a beautiful house, Anne.

ANNE. It is a nice house. I like it.

FREDDIE. It's a professor's house . . . Come up in the world since your little wooden hut by the river . . .

ANNE. I loved that summer house . . .

CROONER.
>You'll see a smiling face,
>A fireplace, a cosy room.
>A little nest that nestles where
>The roses bloom.

HALDER (*to himself*): Life is sweet. . . . For the next five minutes . . .

FREDDIE. Johnnie . . . I want to talk to you . . . Come over here a minute.

HALDER. Anne's cooking a duck for dinner . . . Specially for you . . .

FREDDIE. Good woman . . . Christ, she's an excellent woman you've got, Johnnie . . . You want to hear the verdict . . . The verdict is we can't have any kids . . .

HALDER. That's only one opinion, Freddie, for Christ's sake . . .

FREDDIE. Johnnie, don't be nice to me, not just now . . . Do not be nice to me . . .

HALDER. Nothing marvellous about kids, anyway . . .

FREDDIE. I said don't be nice to me. I know you're a good nice man . . .

HALDER. I mean it . . . There's nothing marvellous about having kids . . .

FREDDIE. You can say that because you've got fucking kids . . . (*Tearing up paper, to stuff in the fire.*) It's a good paper the *Frankfurter Zeitung* for lighting fires. Some papers are better than others . . .

HALDER. Yes, you're right. I used to dream about having a kid, before I had any. You're right.

FREDDIE. Look at us, for fuck's sake. Liz and me . . . They keep on at me at Headquarters . . . When are you going to start fucking breeding. A perfect Nordic pair like you and Liz.

This regime . . . It's obsessed with fucking breeding.

I'm going to be stuck major . . . You know that . . . I might even be demoted . . . Till I breed some fucking kids . . . That's not why *we* want kids . . . That's the official line . . .

I even had to go to Liz's uncle's doctor . . . In Wiesbaden, for fuck's sake . . . Just in case they tracked down my report . . . They'll probably still track it down . . . What am I going to do, for Christ's sake . . . We love each other. You know that . . .

HALDER. It could be the doctor's wrong, Freddie. (*To the audience:*) What else can you say in a situation like that . . . I was getting to love him . . . And Liz . . . We both were . . .

FREDDIE. I haven't been sleeping three nights running. Going round in circles . . . Talking about it . . . Liz and me . . .

CROONER.
>You see a smiling face
>A fireplace
>A cosy room
>A little nest that
>Nestles where
>The roses bloom.
>Just you and me
>And my baby makes three
>In my blue heaven.

FREDDIE. It's *me*. Nothing to do with potency . . . That's all right as far as that's concerned . . . I used to think that was all that counted . . . Liz is all right . . .

HALDER (*to the audience*): Then there was this screaming motorbike. They were always running around with screaming motor bikes . . . With despatch riders . . . Anne showed a young lad into the room . . . Tall . . . blond . . . beautiful in his S.S. uniform . . . He didn't say anything . . . Handed Freddie a sealed envelope.

FREDDIE. All right. Thank you. Dismiss. Heil Hitler . . .

BOY. Heil Hitler . . . The Jews have shot Von Rath, sir. In the Paris Embassy . . .

FREDDIE. Dismiss . . .

BOY. You're to go to headquarters.

FREDDIE. I've got a car.

BOY. Yes, sir . . . (*Going.*)

FREDDIE (*after him*). Von who?!

BOY. A secretary in the Embassy . . . A polish Jew shot him.
   (*He goes.*)

FREDDIE (*reading his orders to* HALDER): If I got desperate . . .
   If you were desperate . . . For your wife to have a kid . . .
   Would you get someone like that lad there . . . ?

HALDER. Who's Von Rath?

FREDDIE. Who the fuck knows or cares. Some fifteenth fucking
   secretary in the Paris Embassy . . . But the cunt's fucked up
   my whole night . . . I haven't had duck for months . . . I
   wanted to fucking talk to you . . .

HALDER. Leave Liz here . . .

FREDDIE. I'll leave Liz here . . . (*To the women*:) Women . . .
   I've got to burn down a few synagogues and arrest some Jews.
   I could be up all night.

ANNE. I thought it was all finished. I thought they'd finished with
   the bloody Jews.

HALDER. A Jew's shot somebody in the Paris Embassy.

FREDDIE (*embracing* LIZ). You stay the night here . . . All right,
   Liz? . . . You'll be all right?

ANNE. You're not really going to burn down synagogues, Freddie?

FREDDIE. Save some of the duck, Anne . . . Won't be the same
   heated up . . . Still . . .

   . . . No . . . First thing is a briefing session to organise, down
   to the last detail, a spontaneous demonstration of the
   indignation of the people of Germany — for tomorrow
   night . . .

OFFICER. Over-Leader Eichmann is ready to see you now,
   Professor Halder . . .

HALDER (*going to* EICHMANN). Thank you . . .
(*To* EICHMANN:) Heil Hitler . . .

EICHMANN. Heil Hitler . . . Sit down Herr Professor . . . I've just
been going through your papers . . . Joined us in 1933 . . .

HALDER. Early 1933, Over-Leader . . .

EICHMANN. And been an excellent comrade, Halder, since
your first days . . . As an officer and a university man.

. . . I think we can work well together . . . The ingredients are
all there . . . For an excellent working relationship . . . What
do you think?

HALDER. If the Leadership believe we can . . .

EICHMANN. You haven't written specifically on the Jewish
Question . . . Halder?

HALDER. My field, as you'll see, is German literature . . .

EICHMANN. I mean on the question from a racial point of
view . . . At the same time, some of your papers here . . . And
reports on some of your lectures . . . This paper on the
reactionary, individual centred emphasis of the Jewish
influence on Western literature . . . Very good, true, deep
comment . . . first class.

HALDER. I have to warn you, Over-Leader, I have had very
little personal contact with Jews . . .

EICHMANN. There's a note here referring to some kind of
friendship with a Gluckstein . . . Maurice Gluckstein . . .

HALDER. Mainly a professional relationship . . . As a doctor . . .

EICHMANN. That's right . . . He was a doctor . . . I have it down
here . . . But your paper on the corrupting Jewish influence
on our literature . . .

HALDER (*turning to students*). I do not wish to get lost in
speculation about such things as Jewish humanist writers'
word orders . . . Or Heine's poetry . . . reflecting the structure
of the Jewish palate . . .

Whether this is objectively true or not seems, to me, trivial
beside the consideration of the direction Judeo-Humanistic

philosophy has pushed Western literature . . .

There is a Talmudic quotation much used by Jewish writers and thinkers: 'If I am not for myself, then who is for me?'

In certain aspects . . . of course, this is a valid question or statement . . . It is, however, in complete contradiction with the basic philosophical statement which is the foundation of the Third Reich: *The common interest before self.*

In the course of these lectures, we will examine the highly individually centred philosophy of Judaism. The concept that God himself can be appealed to directly, without the need for priests or other intermediaries . . . We will look into the evolution from the basic individualistic philosophy — or degeneration — whichever we decide is the case at the end of our investigation — in the total preoccupation with self-fulfilment of much contemporary literature, influenced as it has been by the strong current of Jewish humanism . . . Proust . . . Kafka . . . Freud.

It will be my thesis, that while this was a valid exploration of the human soul at the time, it pushed Western literature in a direction which almost entirely ignored man as a social animal. Man as an organism which, in fact, has no objective reality, no meaning, unless seen in relationship to his culture, the political and economic structure of the society he lives in and so on.

This is not to say that writers have not touched on these aspects of humanity, but they have examined them only from the point of view of individual fulfilment, rather than the fulfilment of a culture, or a nation as a whole.

The question I will be asking, is, can this be the only role of literature? The self-fulfilment of the individual?

Can we not move in a new direction, reflecting that in which our political philosophy has moved . . . *The common interest before self.*

Slow movement of Mendelssohn's violin concerto.

HALDER (*takes a spade. To the audience*): In the morning of

'The Night of Broken Glass', I didn't have to go into the
university . . . I went into the garden to dig the last of the
potatoes. The air was sharp and all the scents of autumn were
still fresh to me. Giving me the feeling I was in a different
country . . .

This Jew operation tonight. It weighed on me . . . along with
the food I couldn't digest properly . . . I enjoyed the
duck . . . at the same time . . .

(*To himself:*) I am very happy. I love her. She loves me. I've
got enough money. People recognise me for the brilliant man
I am . . . Maurice came into the garden, playing Mendelssohn's
violin concerto . . . (*To* MAURICE:) It's a very Jewish
interpretation, Maurice . . . Of course . . . It's a Jewish
concerto . . . That's true.

Listen . . . This Jewish operation tonight . . . If you try to
look at it in perspective . . . Yes . . . Of course . . . It's not a
good thing . . . For tonight . . . and next week . . . Coming
down on a racial group like . . . Arresting Jews . . . Breaking
into their houses and synagogues . . . No doubt — I'll be
honest with you Maurice — kicking in quite a number of Jews'
teeth and balls . . . You know the roughnecks in the Party . . .
Excesses are bound to happen . . .

I am not deluding myself . . . am I? Maurice? This is a regime
in its childhood . . . It's social experiment in its earliest
stages . . . You know what a child is like . . . Self-discipline
isn't formed, yet a large element of unpredictability . . . It
could be . . . if the Jews stayed here much longer . . . You
see what I'm getting at . . . ? Some of the extreme elements
in the regime, could get out of hand . . . Christ knows *what*
they would do to the Jews next . . .

I see tonight . . . As a basically humane action . . . It's going
to shock the Jews into the *reality* of their situation in Nazi
Germany . . . Tomorrow morning . . . They'll be running for
their lives out of the country.

. . . A sharp, sudden shock . . . that is going to make those
who still delude themselves they can stay here in peace to
face reality . . . and . . .

The music stops.

Keep out of it . . . As much as possible. You can do fuck all about it. Tonight . . . what can I do about it? All over the country, they'll be marching against the Jews.

It's a bad thing. No question about it.

Work it out . . . Me . . . If I *died*. That would worry me . . . The idea of being snuffed out . . . If I got *cancer*. That would worry me. Or if they stuck me in one of these concentration camps and one of Himmler's perverts got at me . . . That worries me . . . If Anne stopped loving me and ran off with another man . . . that would worry me.

I've got a whole scale of things that could worry me . . . The Jews and their problems . . . Yes, they are on it . . . but very far down, for Christ's sake . . . Way down the scale. That's not so good, the Jews being so low down on my anxiety scale.

Emotionally. Intellectually . . .

As an intellectual concept it's fairly high as a moral problem . . . The thing is, I am fundamentally a happy person . . . That's what it is . . .

That's the problem. I'm a happy person . . . Absolutely . . .

HALDER's MOTHER, *now in a state of senile dementia, is wheeled out in a wheelchair.*

We're growing marrows in the garden, mother. Dad loved marrows . . . Fried with sausage and onion. That time we went to Rugen . . . Remember that holiday house we had in Rugen . . .

Listen, I have had a complaint about you . . . From the sister . . . Climbing out of your bed in the middle of the night . . . What do you say, mother? . . . I can't make you out . . . (*At last understanding.*) You were going home . . . Yes . . . I understand you, mother . . . I heard you . . . You were going home . . .

BOK (*calling*). Herr Professor . . . It's Bok . . .

HALDER. I'm here . . . Out in the garden . . .

BOK. What a house you've got. A mansion. Look at the garden
  . . . Acres.

HALDER. Four acres.

BOK. You deserve it. I'm delighted for you. Do you know that?
  That you've got a good woman like Frau Halder . . . and a
  house like this.

HALDER. I've got some beer. Would you like some beer, chilled
  in the fridge?

BOK. They sent me up with orders for you. I've got them here.
  I wouldn't mind a cold beer.

HALDER (*to himself*): If they won't let me alone, they won't . . .

BOK. It's a big show tonight. You heard? The Jew cunts
  murdered Von Rath.

HALDER. Was he a friend of yours Bok?

BOK. I like that, that's to the point, isn't it . . . That's a
  wonderful thing about you Herr Professor. You can get it
  straight up the hole . . .

  HALDER *gives him beer.*

  . . . Who gives a shit for Von Rath. You're right. It's the idea
  of a Jew having the cheek to shoot a German.

HALDER. Your beer all right?

BOK. I've never had a garden . . . I thought about getting an
  allotment . . . Never got down to it . . .

HALDER (*reading the orders*). We move into action 3 p.m. this
  afternoon.

BOK. That's the orders. You should see the excitement in the
  university . . . The students are making banners . . . organising
  torches . . . Nobody's doing a stroke of work.

HALDER. I was looking for a peaceful day in the garden. I wish
  they'd get these bloody Jews out of their system. Why didn't
  they all get to hell out of here years ago, while they still had
  a chance.

BOK. Get the cunts out now, Professor.

HALDER. Would that make you really happy, Bok? When there is not a single Yid left in the universe?

BOK. *Me?*

HALDER. I'm talking about *you?* Would that make you really happy . . . Paradise . . . A Jew free world . . ?

BOK. I'll put it to you this way.

Hitler, now . . . he comes up with this stuff about the Jews. He's thought about it, worked it out. The Jews are sucking the fucking lifeblood of the country . . .

Now . . . look at us . . . now . . . He's begun to shake the cunts out. Everybody's got jobs. Holidays . . . Couple of years time, and everybody'll have their own cars. Ordinary workers . . .

Some people used to say he doesn't know what the fuck he's talking about, Hitler . . . Just farts out of his mouth instead of his arsehole.

What do they know? He's delivered the goods, hasn't he? He knew what he was talking about all along.

Herr Professor . . . *You* didn't like living in a Jew Germany . . . Did you? Now . . . You walk about in the streets. And you feel it . . . You know this is *our* place now . . . Don't you? He's got us back our own country . . .

Look at *you,* if you don't mind me saying. You're laughing, now, Professor . . . You've taken over that Jew shit Mandelstam's job . . . big house . . . The whole university's back to a German university . . . You've got no complaints, what Hitler's done for you . . . have you?

HALDER (*to himself*): I am very happy . . .

I am . . .

EICHMANN. Basically, your usual, clear objective reports . . . That's what we want from you, Halder . . . On leadership, morale . . . amenities . . . the general situation of the camps I've listed. I'll follow this up by a personal visit.

HALDER. This order, Over-Leader, to re-settle all the Jews by the end of the year . . .

EICHMANN. Sooner if possible . . .

HALDER. Since we're going to work closely together . . . and I
am in the role of some kind of adviser . . . could I ask you
how you feel about this direction of resources . . . personally
. . . I'm thinking of us fighting the war on so many fronts
. . . the desperate shortage of rolling stock for the offensive
and so on . . . and re-directing so much of it to transporting
Jews . . .

EICHMANN. Russia, we'll soon finish off . . . They're on their
last legs, Halder . . . That'll be one front less . . . In any
case . . . that's our orders . . .

HALDER. I was curious about the need for such urgency . . .

EICHMANN. Your point about fighting on so many fronts . . .
All the more reason to keep the enemy within under tight
control . . . You can see that can't you . . . From the
question of security alone . . .

. . . You'll make the arrangements then . . . You'll need to
base yourself in Berlin during your assignment with me . . .

HALDER. I'll make the arrangements . . . Yes . . .

EICHMANN. The leadership, of course, have ordered me that
on no account are you to cut yourself totally off from your
university . . . Some sabbatical is being arranged for you . . .
But it is vital you are in Berlin within the next week . . . I
look forward to us working together . . .

ANNE. Johnnie . . . Are you going to get changed, for God's
sake . . . You've to report at three o'clock . . .

HALDER (*putting away his spade*). I'm coming.

ANNE. John . . . relax . . . All right, love?

HALDER. I had the picture in my mind, out there in the
garden . . . Germany's been turned into one great prison . . .

You don't think we should run away? It mightn't *be* too late . . .

ANNE. Too late for what? Run away where? Why do you have
to make such a dramatic thing out of everything . . .

HALDER. No . . . Just sometimes I panic . . .

ANNE. I know . . . Now listen here, that's exactly what you are doing. You're panicking . . . Talking about prisons and running away . . . (*Aware of him for the moment in his underwear.*)

. . . Men look funny in their underwear, don't they?

HALDER. Do I?

Yes . . . I panic . . . Sometimes.

In the garden, after Bok went off. I had this wave of panic and guilt . . . I'd destroyed your whole life.

ANNE. How have you done that? If it is destroyed . . . The *words* you use, love! If it is, *I* did it myself. It was *my* choice. *You* . . . I wish you hadn't a wife and other children that keep pulling you from me . . . But you have. I love you. It would've been easier if I loved somebody without all these weights on them . . . But I love *you*.

(*Helping him on with his S.S. uniform.*) What exactly are you going to do tonight? Think about it . . . You're going out on a police action. That's all. You're not going to *shoot* Jews . . . do any violence to them. Your orders are to keep things under control. Stop people burning down Frankfurt . . . That's *all*, for God's sake . . . Just try and think calmly what you are really doing . . .

HALDER. I am. You've got a good logical mind. That's good. You're right.

ANNE. Somebody in the family needs to have one.

Are you going to stop beating your breast now about things you don't *need* to beat your breast about? You've got plenty of *real* things to feel guilty about.

HALDER. You're right. What real things? . . .

ANNE. In any case, for God's sake . . . If I was Jewish I'd have got out of here *years* back . . . The first year Hitler was in power . . . Any Jew with sense is out by now . . . The ones that are left must be utterly stupid or desperate to hang on to their property . . . What are they doing staying in Germany?

HALDER. Listen. You're so clever. You're right. Everything you say is so logical and true.

ANNE. You look lovely in that uniform. I think Elisabeth is after you. Do you know that?

HALDER (*fastening his holster belt*). So we won't run away, then? To California.

ANNE. All right. We'll run away. I'll pack, and you can 'phone your children and tell them you'll write to them every week.

HALDER. I'd better go.

ANNE (*putting his cap on*). Is the revolver loaded?

HALDER. I *think* so.

ANNE. I'll see you when I see you, love.

HALDER. I love you.

ANNE. I love you . . . And no *prisons* or yawning chasms in front of you . . .

HALDER. God, I love you sweetheart . . .

ANNE. I know you do . . .

EICHMANN. What do we do with them, Halder? The sick and the diseased . . . The volume of Jews and anti-socials flooding into the camps . . .

HALDER. I see . . . Yes . . . We're talking about the sick and diseased . . .

EICHMANN. The Reich Leader has been into this personally . . . It is coming from him . . . We need a centre in the east to carry out these actions that are now necessary. . .

HALDER. We are concerned particularly, of course, with the highly infectious diseases . . . Typhoid . . .

EICHMANN. Halder, we're at war. Surrounded by enemies. How can anyone expect us to bear the burden of millions of diseased, anti-socials, sucking the blood and strength of the country . . .

HALDER. I'm looking at the map. I see . . . Because of the railway?

EICHMANN. It's a logical centre . . . We have psychologists and medical doctors and other specialists looking into this. But you are one of us, John . . .

I need a report I can trust . . . An evaluation of the recommendations for the processing of the diseased and the unfit . . . We're not monsters, for God's sake . . . The order's out. It has to be obeyed . . .

I am in total agreement with it, in any case. But I want the same human, without sentimentality approach that seems to be your particular strength . . .

Understood, then?

HALDER. I'll be on the train for Silesia tonight.

EICHMANN. Total and absolute top secret.

I agree, by the way, totally with your report on the accidents in the east. The procedure is not to be even considered. On grounds of humanity, among other things.

I want any evidence you might find there, too, of unnecessary cruelty . . . indulgence in sadistic behaviour . . . Apart from anything else, these things have a disastrous effect on the general level of discipline . . .

HALDER. I'll make a full report.

EICHMANN. Directly to me. No copies, Halder!

HALDER. Maurice came to me. With the Frankfurt Jewish Male Voice Choir (singing 'Jesu Joy of Man's Desiring'). He had disappeared months ago. I don't know where to. One day he stopped meeting me in the park. But he came to me that night. Through the smoke of the burning buildings.

MAURICE. The flames are aesthetic. Never seen Frankfurt look more like the set of 'Götterdämmerung' at Bayreuth.

HALDER (*to the audience*): It was five o'clock in the morning and they were still at it. I was dizzy with the smoke and the violence was getting to my nerves.

We were sitting on a scrap of wasteland. Although it was November, there was still flowers growing through the cracks in the concrete.

(*To* MAURICE:) Maurice . . . It's just come to me . . . Our whole approach has been superficial and simplistic . . . The *Jews* the Victims — the *Nazis* the Persecutors . . . We've reduced the whole complex situation to this stock, simplistic construct. (MAURICE *takes this in*.) What do you think, Maurice?

MAURICE. I'm trying to take it in, Johnnie. The effect seems simple enough . . . They mow me down with machine-guns, cut off my balls, rape my wife . . . no . . . I take that back . . . Most of the cunts couldn't rape a fucking sparrow.

HALDER. What we are doing, Maurice . . . listen to this . . . is we are allowing ourselves to be trapped by obvious, stock responses . . . Instead of daring to confront ourselves with reality maybe, Maurice, maybe . . . It's the Jews' fault . . . They are responsible for pushing Germany into this Jewish, moralistic, humanistic, Marxist total fuck up . . .

MAURICE *goes back to his choir*.

Maurice . . . I'm trying to communicate deep and profound truths with you . . . Will you stop conducting that choir . . . What is the Frankfurt Jewish Male Choir doing singing about Jesus, anyway . . .

MAURICE. It's reformed. Converted . . .

HALDER. No. I withdraw the word 'profound'. I accept that. Profundity has nothing to do with human beings . . . Whenever you imagine yourself soaring to profundity, remember the total balaity of your existence and vision.

MAURICE. That's true. That's a profound statement, Johnnie . . .

HALDER (*watching the flames*). You think we might be having a nervous breakdown. The whole thing is a national nervous breakdown?

MAURICE. It's standard process. Evolution, isn't it? Animals go as far along the line of development as they can. And that's it. They become too big or too heavy . . . or too specialised . . . and they go extinct . . . Don't worry about it . . .

HALDER. I don't accept that . . .

MAURICE. All right. Don't accept it. Please yourself.

HALDER. Maurice. We have to accept the consequences of your
Jewish Humanism . . . The time's past for covering it up with
pseudo-scientific smokescreens . . . I'm not blaming you . . .
I forgive you, Maurice.

MAURICE. What's he saying? What is this shithead talking about?
It's my fault, his fucking machine-guns mowed me down?

HALDER. I'm talking about objective moral truth, Maurice.

What is an Objective Moral Truth? I'm not being profound,
Maurice . . . I'm just coming to grips with reality . . . What
has happened, is we have confused subjective fantasy concepts
like good, bad, right, wrong, human, inhuman . . . as objective,
immutable laws of the universe.

Jews are bad, Germas are good . . . Like a stone falls to the
ground . . . It is a moral act to get rid of the Jews. It's an
immoral act . . . That's the kind of clouded, subjective
thinking parading as objective truth that has totally disorientated
the world and led us into this violence and chaos . . . There's
something there, Maurice . . . Do you think there's something
there?

MAURICE. I'm confused . . . What are you saying! It's a good
thing to have your balls cut off . . . It's a beautiful, uplifting
experience being mowed down by machine-guns . . . Johnnie
I'm confused . . .

HALDER. It's what is happening. That is what human beings
do . . . What happens. How the world is. Not what Jesus or
Lenin or Moses or all the Jewish moralists would like it to be.
How it is . . . If we could work on that basis of accepting the
world *as it is* . . . What do you think?

MAURICE. People fuck other people's wives, Johnnie . . . That's
the world *as it is*. How does that fit in with your new approach,
Boychical?

HALDER. That's true . . . That's an important point . . . I don't
like that . . . The idea of somebody stealing Anne . . . That's

not good, Maurice. You're right . . .

MAURICE. Listen. Don't worry about it . . . It's too complicated.
There's too many people in the world to cope with . . . With
too many problems.

HALDER. Coping with all these *people*, Maurice.

MAURICE. Two's difficult . . . Three's getting too many . . .
Ten for a Minyan's impossible . . .

HALDER. Listen . . . You're probably right, Maurice . . . The
way things are going . . . That should be the end of us . . .
You're right . . . I can't see people lasting much longer on this
earth . . .

MAURICE. Best thing. A finish to people torturing the earth.
I'm telling you. Who needs us?

Look at that — what is it? Ragwort? — Dandelion? Pushing
its way through solid concrete.

MAURICE. Through a crack.

HALDER. That's right. It couldn't push it's way through
concrete.

MAURICE. Concrete rots in the end. It can wait.

HALDER. It can wait. Plants are in no hurry.

MAURICE. John my friend, let's go home.

HALDER. You know what I could do with? A good thick slice
of ham . . . two eggs . . . black bread and butter . . . hot mug
of coffee . . . and seeing Anne . . . could do with my arms
round Anne more than anything else just now.

MAURICE. Let it all burn. Don't want to drag out the end too
long.

HALDER (*bending to the flower*). So don't worry, ragwort or
whatever you are . . . Won't be long, now . . . You'll soon
have it all to yourself.

(*To* MAURICE *as they go* :) Nice flower that, Maurice.

They walk towards ANNE, *waiting for them.* ANNE *goes to*
HALDER *with his greatcoat . . . helps him on with it.*

ANNE. We're mad. Some couples are separated for years . . .

HALDER. I know.

ANNE. I've never heard of Auschwitz.

HALDER. In Upper Silesia . . .

ANNE. Yes, you told me . . .

HALDER. I should be back in a week or so . . . Two at the most . . . I'll 'phone you every day, if I can.

ANNE. There is something wrong with us . . . The way we can't stand being separated . . .

HALDER. I know . . .

ANNE. Are you all right, now, love?

HALDER. I'm fine . . .

ANNE. John . . . listen to me . . . Whatever happens . . . round us . . . However we get pushed . . . I know we're good people . . . both of us . . . It just isn't what's happened . . . You destroyed me . . . Pulled me down . . . It isn't . . . It's the other way round . . . You've pulled me up . . . I've done the same for you . . . From the first time we came together . . .

HALDER. Yes . . . We probably are . . . *good* . . . Yes . . . Whatever that means . . .

ANNE. You know what it means.

HALDER. Yes . . .

ANNE. *Remember* it then.

HALDER (*to the audience*): I got into Auschwitz early in the morning. It was an ordinary dirty industrial town. Big station. Munition trains . . . sparrows on the platform poking at microscopic crumbs on the concrete. People going about their work. Like a normal town.

I was sitting on the platform, feeling insecure like I always feel away from home . . . absolutely longing for Anne and the children . . . the comfort of her hand in mine.

I'd taken out a book, while I was waiting for a car from the camp to pick me up. A German translation of *Don Quixote* . . .

I could only read escapist literature like that in these days . . .

ANNE. Remember it, then. And remember that I love you. And you love me . . . and we'll always love one another . . . Will you remember that . . .

HALDER (*kissing her eyelids*). I'll remember that.

Music: Schubert march.

(*To the audience:*) When we arrived at the camp, Höss, the Commandant, was waiting at the gate for me.

HÖSS *comes forward.*

(*To the audience as he shakes hands with* HÖSS:) Funny man . . . Poor soul . . . Something *wrong* with him. I was trying to work out what exactly it was, all the time he was welcoming me . . .

HÖSS. That's very kind. Reich Leader Eichmann sending his regards. Of course, please convey mine to him. My very kindest regards.

HALDER (*to the audience*): He showed no emotion. That was it. Might have been some mental condition. On the other hand, just stress . . . The poor bastard had a hell of a job . . . He did make a supreme effort and *smiled.*

The funny thing was . . . I heard this band. Playing a Schubert March. 'Oh,' I registered to myself. 'We're having Schubert, now.'

. . . Then I became aware that there was in fact a group of prisoners . . . maybe in my honour. I'm not sure . . . The important thing was . . . The significant thing: the band was *real.*

Up band . . . HALDER *watching them . . .*

. . . The band was *real!*

Up music.

Appendix

The music for the original production included excerpts from the following.

Title	Composer	Publisher
ACT ONE		
'No Other Love' ('Du bist mein Stern')	Music: Eisemann Mihaly Words: Pam Smalley	Peter Maurice Music Ltd.
'Night in Monte Carlo'	Werner R. Heymann	Copyright unknown
'I'm always chasing Rainbows'	Words: Joseph McCarthy Music: Harry Carroll	Francis Day & Hunter. (Robins Music) EMI.
'September Song'	Words: Maxwell Anderson Music: Kurt Weill	Chappell & Co.
'Star of Eve'	Wagner	
'You Are My Heart's Delight'	Words: Harry Graham Music: Franz Lehar	Chappell & Co.
'Falling in love Again'	Friedrich Holländer	Campbell Connelly & Co. Ltd.
'Bavarian Mt. Band'	George Fenton	
'Jewish Wedding Song'	Trad.	
'Drinking Song' (from *The Student Prince*.)	Words: Dorothy Donnelly Music: Sigmund Romberg	Chappell & Co.
ACT TWO		
'Monte Carlo'	as above	
'Lohengrin' (*Prelude Act Three*)	Wagner	
'I'm always chasing Rainbows'	as above	

Title	Composer	Publisher
'Ständchen' ('Serenade')	Schubert	
'Symphony No. 6'	Beethoven	
'Tannhäuser' (Pilgrims)	Wagner	
'My Blue Heaven'	Words: George Whitling Music: Walter Donaldson	Francis Day & Hunter
'Violin Concerto'	Mendelssohn	
'Lohengrin'	Wagner	
'Jesu Joy of man's Desiring'	Bach	
'March Militaire'	Schubert	
'Carolina in the Morning'		
'My Very Good Friend the Milkman, Said'		

O Jesu, Joy of Man's Desiring

Jesu, joy of man's desiring,
Holy wisdom, love most bright,
Drawn by thee, our souls aspiring,
Soar to uncreated light.

Word of God our flesh that fashion'd
With the fire of life impassion'd
Striving still to truth unknown,
Soaring, dying, round Thy throne.

Drinking Song

Drink! Drink! Drink!
To eyes that are bright as stars when they're shining on me!
Drink! Drink! Drink!
To lips that are red and sweet as the fruit on the tree!

Here's a hope that those bright eyes will shine
Lovingly, longingly, soon into mine!
May those lips that are red and sweet,
Tonight with joy my own lips meet!

Drink! Drink! Let the toast start!
May young hearts never part!
Drink! Drink! Drink!
Let ev'ry true lover salute his sweetheart!
Let's drink!

Drink! Drink! Drink!
To arms that are white and warm as a rose in the sun!
Drink! Drink! Drink!
To hearts that will love one, only when I am the one!

Here's a hope that those soft arms will twine
Tenderly, trustingly, soon around mine!
May she give me a priceless boon:
Her love beneath the sweet May moon!

Drink! Drink! Let the toast start!
May young hearts never part!
Drink! Drink! Drink!
Let ev'ry true lover salute his sweetheart!
Let's drink!

And A Nightingale Sang . . .

To my mother, with love

And A Nightingale Sang . . . was first staged on 10 March 1977 by Live Theatre in Newcastle-on-Tyne in a production directed by Paul Chamberlain.

And A Nightingale Sang . . . was subsequently presented by SRO Productions Limited in the version printed here at the Queen's Theatre, London on 11 July 1979, with the following cast:

HELEN STOTT, *early thirties* — Gemma Jones
JOYCE STOTT, 22, *her sister* — Veronica Sowerby
GEORGE, *fifties, her father* — Arthur Blake
PEGGY (MAM), *fifties, her mother* — Patricia Routledge
ANDIE, *seventy-odd, her grandfather* — Roger Avon
ERIC, *early twenties, Joyce's husband* — Christian Rodska
NORMAN, *early thirties* — Ray Brooks

Directed by Mike Ockrent
Designed by Geoffrey Scott
Lighting by Leonard Tucker
Incidental Music & Supervision Peter Skellern

The action of the play takes place in Newcastle-on-Tyne, during the years of World War Two.

Act One

Scene One

Oh, Johnnie, How You Can Love
Sunday, 3 September 1939

HELEN. That Sunday . . we were too busy to notice the war . . So
many things were happening to us . . . The Coalman, me Da, was
playing 'Oh, Johnnie' . . . . That was me Mam . . She gave everybody
nicknames . . . I was 'The Cripple' . . . Me Granda was 'The Old
Soldier' . . . Our Joyce was 'The Babe in the Wood' . . . We called
our Mam back 'The Saint' . . . .

GEORGE. (singing at the piano).
    Oh, Johnnie,
    Oh, Johnnie,
    How you can love, etc.

HELEN. Me Mam was making Sunday dinner . . . Joyce was making up
her mind to say 'yes' or 'no' to Eric . . . And Granda was getting
ready for Jackie's funeral . . .

ANDIE. (with a sack). You want to see him before we go?

JOYCE. Ee . . . . You haven't brought him in here, Granda . . .

ANDIE. (looking in the sack). He looks lovely . . . Peaceful and
serene . . .

HELEN. He didn't suffer . . . You can see that . . .

ANDIE. Want to look at him George . . .

GEORGE. What do I want to see a bloody dead dog for, man . . . Get
him out.

MAM. Ee . . . You haven't brought him in here . . . Put him in the bin,
man . . . I've put everything in the oven . . Ready . . . . Helen . . .
Are you listening to us?

GEORGE. Where you going *now*, man . . . It's near dinner time . . .

JOYCE. She's going to the chapel . . . .

GEORGE. She's just bloody *come* from the chapel . . .

ANDIE. He was a trier . . . . That was one thing about him . . wasn't
it . . . (*Into the sack.*) Ee . . You were a trier son . .

GEORGE. Never even got a place . . Five years you raced him.

ANDIE. He raced his heart out; Didn't he Helen . . .

MAM. Right . . I'll be back as soon as I can . . .

GEORGE. Where are you going, man?

MAM. Father Monaghan's very upset . . . I told you . . You never
listen to people . . If you'd stop banging away at that bloody
piano . . .

GEORGE. I'm trying to get a chord right . . . Does that sound right . .

MAM. Father Ryan said to us . . This morning . . Coming out from
Mass . . I've told you all this before . .

ANDIE. *Monaghan's* the one that let me down . . . I didn't ask him
to come to the ceremony . . . I wouldn't do that . .

GEORGE. What's he rambling on about, now . . .

ANDIE. I'm talking about the funeral . . . You going to get your coat
on Helen . .

HELEN. I'm coming, Grandad . . .

JOYCE. Mam . . I still don't know what I should do . . . He's coming
for his dinner . . .

MAM. Give him his dinner . . .

ANDIE. I asked Monaghan . . . I've had a bereavement . .

MAM. Where's me bag?

HELEN. Mam, shouldn't you stay here . . . I know Father Monaghan's
bad . . . but Eric's coming . . . and we've had the upset with
Jackie . . .

MAM. You don't know what's been happening up there . . . Father
Monaghan could be losing God and Christ . . Do you know that?

GEORGE. Tell him to put an advert in the Chronicle.

JOYCE. I feel rotten . . Mam . . You know . . Eric going away . . . .

MAM. I can smell that bloody animal . . . . Will you get him *out* of here!

ANDIE. He's only dead a day, man . . There's no smell from him . .

MAM. *(with disinfectant).* Put some of that in the bag . . will you . .

JOYCE. Ee . . I couldn't go near it . . Mam . . .

MAM. *I'll* do it . .

JOYCE. Mam . . . Mam.

ANDIE. What are you doing, man . . . Putting chemicals all over the body . . .

MAM. Get it out, then . . . .

ANDIE. I'm waiting for Helen to get ready . . .

JOYCE. He's bought a ring for us and everything . . . .

MAM. I like him. He's a canny lad . . .

JOYCE. What do *you* think, Dad . . .

GEORGE. I'm just curious . . . I'd like to know . . What does she do there with all them priests . . .

JOYCE. He could be going to his

MAM. If you're interested . . They think he's had a bit of a breakdown . . . Father Monaghan . . .

JOYCE. Mam . . I want to talk to you . . Helen . . Tell us. What do you think I should do . . .

HELEN. *(to* AUDIENCE). I'd been bloody telling her for the last six weeks . . . . Up every night till four o'clock in the morning telling her . . . .

ANDIE. I'm finished with the Catholic Church . . . They've let me down for the last time . . I go to Monaghan . . And say to him . . 'I don't expect you to go to me dog's funeral . .'

MAM. You didn't ask him to bury that mongrel of yours . . .

GEORGE. It's a whippet . . Bitch . . .

ANDIE. . . . . All I want is a few words . . . From the Missall . . To say over the poor soul . . .

MAM. Dogs haven't *got* a soul . . .

ANDIE. You should've heard the mouth that papist parasite opened to us . . .

JOYCE. Mam . . He's bringing the ring . . This morning . .

MAM. Do you not love him? . .

HELEN. She doesn't *know* . . .

JOYCE. I'm frightened . . Mam . . I don't know . . .

MAM. Eee . . I don't know *what* you should do, pet . . I've got to go . . .
He's always liked us . . . There's a bond between us . . . Father
Monaghan and me . . . From the first day he came here . . .

ANDIE. Are *you* coming, Joyce? . . .

MAM. How can she come . . She's waiting for her lad, man . .

ANDIE. It's a poor turn out . . Isn't it . . Two for a funeral . . . After all
that Dog's meant in the house . . Been like a baby . . .

MAM. . . . You see he's been praying for six months and fasting . . .

ANDIE. The last time . . Before we go . . Who wants to bid a last
farewell to Jackie . .

GEORGE. *Goodbye Jackie* . .

ANDIE. *(looking in the sack)*. . . Gives your heart a turn, doesn't it,
Helen . . Looking at him lying there . . He's his eyes open . . He's
had a good life . . . even though he wasn't a winner . . .

MAM. After Mass . . Father Ryan came to us . . .

GEORGE. I still don't understand what she's going to do . . With
Father Monaghan . . . To keep him out of St. Nicks.

MAM. He's not going to St Nicholas . . Don't say that . . . George, man
. . . He's just having a bit of a breakdown . . .

GEORGE. Listen, if ye're going to bury the poor bugger . . Ye want te
mark the spot . . don't ye . . . Here lies Jackie . . Faithful to the
last . . Then some striking memory of him . . .

MAM. Like he was always dirtying the kitchen carpet . . .

ANDIE. You being a Catholic, should know that . . . It's a feature of
all God's creatures . . isn't it . . . They *all* shit . . . Way you can
recognise them from a stone . . . What's the difference between a
stone and a dog . . . One shits . . one doesn't . .

MAM. They don't all do their business on my kitchen carpet . . do
they . .

HELEN (*to* AUDIENCE). They were all kind of stuck there . . . The
Old Soldier with Jackie in his sack . . The Coalman . . At his

piano . . . The Saint . . with her coat on . . . The Babe in the
Wood . . . Making herself up . . just in case she was going to take
him . . . Everybody waiting for me as usual . . . to make up their
minds for them . . . I was just going to take everything in hand as
usual . . . And tell me Mam to go off to the Manse . . . And take
Grandad to Walker with the dog . . . When the doorbell rang . . .
And Joyce went white . . . Dad got up to answer it . . . Mam
stopped him . .

MAM. Wait a minute, man . . . Where you going . .

GEORGE. Going to answer the bloody door . .

JOYCE. It's *him*, Da . . . It's Eric . .

MAM. We haven't decided what's to be done . . . Have we . . .

GEORGE. Ye not think it would be easier just to say 'yes', and get
it over with . . This is bloody worse than Chamberlain running back
and forwards to Germany . . waiting for Hitler to make up his
mind . . *Will* I kick their teeth in . . will I not . . .

JOYCE. I don't know if I love him . .

GEORGE. I don't know if I love yer Mam . . but I'm bloody married
to her . .

MAM. Now . . That's not true . . You know that . . . That's just an
act . . . That's confusing the lass altogether.

The bell rings again.

HELEN. I'll take him in the front room . . You can't leave him at the
door . . . like that . . . till you make up your mind about taking him
or not . . .

JOYCE. Tell him I'm still getting dressed . . .

HELEN (*to* AUDIENCE). Eric was there, all his brasses shining . . .
like he'd been up all night polishing them for the great day . . And
his cap tucked in his epaulets . . .

ERIC. This is it . . . Eh, Helen . . .

HELEN. Is it? What? . . .

ERIC. Be on the wireless. Eleven o'clock . . Chamberlain . . .

HELEN. Joyce is getting dressed . . . Better come in the front room . . .
The kitchen's in a state . .

ERIC. 's alright . . Doesn't bother me . . .

HELEN. You've to come in the front room . . .

ERIC. Okey Dokey . . Front Room . . . Want to see the ring . . .

HELEN. Want a cup of tea?

ERIC. It's a nice ring . . . Got it in Glasgow . . . Going to Fort George for training . . .

HELEN. The Old Soldier's dog's dead . .

ERIC. Is he . . Shame . .

MAM. Helen . . Oh . . Hullo Eric. You're looking very smart . .

ERIC. Got the wireless on, Mrs. Stott . .?

MAM (*to* HELEN). Joyce wants you a minute . .
    (*To* ERIC.) She's just getting dressed . .

ERIC. Be on my way soon . . Mrs. Stott . . .

MAM. You not stopping for a cup of tea . .?

ERIC. I mean . . To fight old Adolf . . .

MAM. I've to go to the Church . . One of the Father's has taken bad . .

ERIC. I'm sorry about that . . Do you want to see the ring . .

HELEN. I'd better see what Joyce wants . .

MAM. I'll get you a cup of tea . . .

HELEN (*to* AUDIENCE). So . . . Eric was left on his own . . . Sitting in the cold sitting room . . . *Nobody* wanting to see his ring . . . Joyce . . was in the bedroom . . .

JOYCE. I don't like him . . Helen . . Do *you* like him . . I looked through the door . . at him coming in . . He smells of *bacon* doesn't he?

HELEN. Send him packing . . If you don't like him . . then . .

JOYCE. Ee . . You don't think I should do that . . . He might be going to his death . . . If I sent him away like that . . . It would be on my conscience the rest of my life . . wouldn't it . . . Just at his hour of need . . . When all I needed to say was one word . . . To make him happy . . . I kept it back . . .

HELEN. Do you *believe* that . . . Joyce . .

JOYCE. He could go away to France, happy . . .

HELEN. Joyce . . Stop it . . will you.

JOYCE. Stop what . . man . .

HELEN. Stop being in a picture . . will you . . .

JOYCE. Do you like me hair this way . . .

HELEN. Not particularly . . .

JOYCE. I'd better change it . . . Helen, what would *you* do?

HELEN (*to* AUDIENCE). What would *I* bloody do . . . I've never had
the chance . . have I? . . . With a face like mine . . and my body all
out of shape . . . If I walked down Shields Road . . naked . . no man
would look at us twice . . . I don't know what I'd do . . . I'd given up
thinking of having somebody to love us . . . I wasn't bothered . . . I
could do *without* bloody men . . Plenty other things to give you a
lift in life . . wasn't there . . . .

JOYCE. I can't even remember the colour of his eyes . . Me Mam says
they're green . . If they're green . . they're unlucky . . aren't they . . .

HELEN. Oh . . For God's sake . . Joyce . . .

JOYCE. Should I put a ribbon in my hair . . . Has he shown you the
ring . . . What it's like . .

HELEN. I haven't had time to look . . .

JOYCE. It's the idea of being tied for life to him . . .

HELEN. Not if he's going to die in France, tomorrow . . Joyce . .

JOYCE. Ee . . . Don't say that . .

HELEN (*to* AUDIENCE). And she went over to the statue of our lady
. . and bloody prayed . . .

JOYCE. . . . Dear Lady of Grace . . Please bring Eric Parker safely
through the war . . . and let him return safe and sound to his
home . . Amen . .

ANDIE. (*at the doorway with his tea*). You can forget about that . .
Joyce . . Time he'll get back from France . . he'll be an old man . .
There's his tea, Helen . . . Everything's been held up . . . I hate
being held up like this . . . I was planning the funeral for ten
o'clock . . You've to take his tea into him . . Yer Mam can't face
him just now . .

HELEN. *You* take it in . .

ANDIE. Every war . . . Gets longer and longer . . . Doesn't it . . .
The Boer War wasn't bad . . . But the 1914 war . . Four years . . .
This one . . . This one . . . I reckon . . . it should last out . . . thirty
or forty years . . . They'll stand there like two champions . .
hammering each other into the ground . .

HELEN. Take Eric's tea in . . . it's getting cold man . .

JOYCE. Ee . . Granda . . . What am I going to do . .

ANDIE. I wouldn't worry about it Joyce . . Come to the funeral with me and the Cripple . . It'll cheer you up . . .

JOYCE. One minute . . I love him . . you see, Granda . . the next I'm not sure . . .

ANDIE. It's like the tide . . you see . . . Human emotions . . They wax and wane . . . like the tide . .

JOYCE. Do they? . .

ANDIE. I don't know . . That's what it said in one of yer Mam's rubbish magazines . . . I read it last week . . . Love ebbs and flows like the tide . . . What's going to happen . . I don't want to frighten you . .

HELEN. Give us the tea . . .

ANDIE. That's right, you take it to him . . . Hitler'll bomb the whole of England . . . There'll be nowt left . . . All of England will be left in France to fight it out . . . Boom . . . Quick end . . . That's us finished . . . Best way when you think about it . . anyway . . What is living . . . Just working out some way of passing the time you're alive . . . in between eating and shitting and sleeping . . . Better to get it over in a flash like it's going to be . . isn't it . . .

HELEN. Give us that tea . .

JOYCE. Helen . . Look at his eyes . . will you . . . What colour do you think Eric's eyes are, Granda? . .

ANDIE. Yer Mam thinks it's green . .

JOYCE. Ee . . They're not . .

ANDIE. Green's her unlucky colour . . . I told her . . . If you believe it's unlucky . . It's unlucky . . . Keep off green . . . If you believe in it . . . it's true . .

HELEN (*to* AUDIENCE). I hadn't any time for the Old Soldier when he started on that analysing life thing . . . I went into Eric with his tea . . He was getting a bit impatient . . .

   (*To* ERIC.) A watched kettle . . Never boils . .

ERIC. You want to see the ring . . Helen . .

HELEN. She's nearly ready . . What colour's your eyes . .

ERIC. Never looked . .

HELEN. Kind of brown . . Or could just be olive green . .

ERIC. Never thought about it . . . That's the ring . .

HELEN. It's nice . . *(Not looking at it.)* . . Your tea alright . .?

ERIC. I got it off a bloke in the pub. It's a quarter carat . . . Worth a lot of money . . Course I didn't ask him where *he* got it . . . Nice isn't it . . .

HELEN. So you're off to France . .

ERIC. Not allowed to say where we're going . . In case the Germans get to know . . Spies . . You know . . . She nearly ready . . .? I'm going to Morpeth . . . Longhorsley — near Morpeth for training.

HELEN. You're *not* going to France . .?

ERIC. Not tomorrow . . Will . . you know . . when it's time . . Where you going?

HELEN. I forgot to get you a biscuit . . *(Going to* JOYCE.) He's not going to France . . .

MAM. Thank God . . . and the Sacred Heart . . for answering me prayers . .

JOYCE. Thank you, Dear Lady . . .

HELEN. He's going to Morpeth . . .

MAM. Ee . . What a relief . . . I'd better get to the Manse then . .

JOYCE. Mam, wait a minute, man . . . What should I do? . .

HELEN. He's not going to his death for a month or so . . till he's finished his training . . .

JOYCE. Did you see the ring . . . What's it like?

HELEN. It's a half a carat diamond solitaire . . Looks nice enough . .

JOYCE. Ee . . Is it . . .

MAM. What colour's his eyes . . They're green . . aren't they . .

HELEN. Brown . . Brownish green . . Olive green . . I don't know . . Pink . . .

JOYCE. What do you think about this ribbon . .

MAM. It's nice, pet . . It's understandable . . . If a priest has prayed night and day and fasted . . . for peace . . . and then this happens . . . It's a trial to his faith . . . .

HELEN. I'd better take him in a biscuit . . and you'd better come in and talk to him right away . . . .

(*To* AUDIENCE.) In the sitting room . . The Coalman was entertaining Eric . . Now . . Playing the Last Post . . on his mouth organ . . . .

(*To* ERIC.) She's nearly ready . . . .

ERIC. Okey dokey . . . Do you want to see the ring, Mr. Stott . .

HELEN. Would it not be in your Army Card . . . Your eye colour . . .

ERIC. Would it?

GEORGE. I think for myself . . . Always have thought for myself . . . I don't let any man dictate to me what I should think . . . About Hitler or anything else . . . . I mean . . You can see Hitler's point about the Poles . . Going into Poland . . . Very dodgy people, the Poles . . . Swychinsky . . . Ted Swychinsky . . . Know him?

ERIC. I don't know him . . .

HELEN. Let's see your card, Eric . .

GEORGE. He stole my horse . . Put us out of business . . 1937 . . . .

ERIC. Sorry to hear that, Mr. Stott . . .

GEORGE. You had to change your horses when I was in the coal trade . . winter . . spring . . Sold the spring horse . . and bought a heavier one for winter . . other way round spring . . . I was bad with me chest . . That spring . . Swychinsky . . my mate . . Says: I'll take the horse to market . . . . £22 . . Reserve . . . I'm showing you the kind of character your Pole is . .

ERIC. Got it . . . (*with the card.*)

HELEN. Does it say . .?

ERIC. Looking . . .

GEORGE. Does a deal outside the ring . . Seventeen quid . . Pockets it . . and runs off to Middlesbrough with the seventeen quid . . drinks and whores it till its done . . . That's me out of the coal trade . . No horse . . . Finished . . That's the Poles for you . . .

ERIC. It says . . Olive Green . .

HELEN. Does it . . .

MAM. She wants you again. (*To* ERIC.) She got a stain on her dress and had to change it . .

HELEN. I'd better go to her . .

(*To* AUDIENCE.) Joyce was writing a letter . .

JOYCE. I'm writing to him, Helen . . . I'm writing him a nice letter.

HELEN. Send him a telegram, man . . It'll be quicker.. .

JOYCE. Don't start getting sarky with us, Helen . . Just now . . That'll finish us altogether . . .

MAM. Is she nearly ready . . .

HELEN. You go off to Father Monaghan . . Mam . . It's alright . .

MAM. Ee . . I *couldn't* . . And leave everything on you . .

ANDIE. Are we *going*? . .

MAM. Will you get him out of here . . Joyce is changing . . .

JOYCE. . . . Dear Eric, It is easier to say this in a letter . . .

HELEN (*to* AUDIENCE). And at that minute, Hitler turned up . . Mam was just saying . .

MAM. What I might do is nip out for a minute . . to tell them I'll be held up going to see the Father . . What do you think Helen . . (*Sirens.*)

ANDIE. Christ! The Bloody Germans . .

HELEN (*to* AUDIENCE). Ee . . That miserable sound . . Everybody turned white . . . It had us trembling . . I don't know what it was . . It was the first time in my life . . I'd been really terrified . . .

MAM. What are we going to do Helen . . What are we going to do . . .

GEORGE. It's the bloody sirens . . . You hear them . . .

MAM. George . . What are we going to do . . .

GEORGE. What's Joyce doing . .

HELEN. She's writing a letter . . .

(*To* AUDIENCE.) And then Eric came in . . and completely took over . .

ERIC. Get your gas masks . . Hullo Joyce . .

JOYCE. Hullo Eric . . I was just writing to you . . .

ERIC. Get your gas mask, man . . .

JOYCE. I'll get it Eric . . .

ERIC. Everybody get your gas masks . . . We've been told . . The first time they come over . . they'll probably drop gas . . to surprise us . . Better get into the kitchen . . .

HELEN (*to* AUDIENCE). He pushed us all into the kitchen . . . and started stuffing towels and that into the cracks in the door . . .

MAM. (*with her mask.*) Eric . . What are we going to do . . These things don't work . . Do they? . .

ERIC. Seal up all the doors . . .

ANDIE. I've got to get to Walker Park, Eric, man . . to bury me dog! . . .

ERIC. Put that fire out, somebody . .

MAM. What are you looking for now man . .

GEORGE. Where's last night's chronicle . . It's in the Chronicle . . . What to do in air raids . .

ERIC. I know what to do in air raids, Mr. Stott . . . Get your gas mask . . .

GEORGE. I'm checking for meself . . .

ERIC. Will you get your gas mask, Mr. Ryan . .

ANDIE. There's nothing to worry about, son . . . We are here . . by a mistake . . . An accident . . .

MAM. For God's sakes, Da . . . Don't start that, now . . (*To* ERIC.) You're putting out the fire . .

ERIC. That's right . . . Get us some blankets . .

ANDIE. If we die, we die. It's not as deadly as people think dying.

GEORGE. Where's me bloody *chronicle,* man . . .

MAM. I think I cut it up . . . It's in the netty . . . Where's he going . . . Stop him . .

GEORGE. I'm going to get me Chronic . . .

MAM. You'll get bombed, George man . . Stay where you are . . .

ERIC. The planes might take a bit to get here . . . We'll hear them . . . First thing we'll hear . . . is the Anti-Aircraft guns going off . .

JOYCE. Is that what you hear first Eric . .

ERIC. That's what you hear first . . .

GEORGE. (*returning with the Chronicle*). You're pretty sharp, aren't you . . Using me Chronicle for netty paper . . aren't you . . . I don't know *where* it is, now . . . Eric . . man . . That's a good blanket . . . Stop him man . . Stuffing a good blanket like that up the chimney . . .

ERIC. Keeping the gas out, aren't we . . .

ANDIE. I'm telling you, let it in, man . . And finish it off once and for all . . .

MAM. Ee . . Do you think poor Father Monaghan's going to survive all this, Helen? . . .

JOYCE. Will I help you, Eric . .

ANDIE. Work it out for yourselves . . People's like a disease . . on the earth . . . That's what I'm talking about . .

GEORGE. I've got it . . . This man was out in Spain . . and was in dozens of air raids . . . It says you don't need to worry about air raids . . .

ANDIE. That's what I'm talking about . . . Listen . . . You get born . . . right . . You grow up . . . You hang around . . all your life . . . Grafting your life away . . . What for? . . .

ERIC. No planes yet?

JOYCE. Are there not . .

GEORGE. (reading). I have been in dozens of air raids . . . People think air raids are worse than they really are . . Believe me . . If you take the proper precautions . . You can survive the worst raid . .

ANDIE. You end up losing your teeth . . your hair . . everything . . . waiting for your time to come . . . What's the point . . . Take Jackie . . . Died in his prime . . . With all his faculties . .

HELEN. Granda, Sit down, man . . . And take it easy . . .

ANDIE. I'm telling you . . . We'd be doing everybody a good turn . . . Getting the earth clean of a disease . . People . . Digging into it . . . burning it . . . Killing all the animals . . . You should've seen Flanders when we left it . . 1917 . . . .

GEORGE. When you hear the planes coming . . Throw yourself on the ground . .

ERIC. That's just when you've no cover, Mr. Stott . .

GEORGE. Are you trying to argue with a man who has been through dozens of air raids . . .

ANDIE. Not a tree left standing . . . Everything flattened . . not a bit of green . . the whole earth churned up . . . I'm telling you . . We're better out of it . . . For everybody's sake . . .

JOYCE. Ee . . I'm frightened, Eric . . .

ERIC. It's all right . . . Got everything organised . . .

JOYCE. If *you* weren't here . . Eric . .

GEORGE. We'd had Hitler jumping through the kitchen window . . . .
Now . . This is important . . Listen to this . .

MAM. I wish you wouldn't read that . . It upsets us . . . Listening to
things like that . . .

GEORGE. The bomb makes a rushing screaming sound as it
approaches . .

MAM. I'm not listening . . . George . . .

GEORGE. As soon as you hear that . . . Get down on the ground . .
Throw yourself on the ground . . .

ANDIE. When you think about it . . He's better out of it, isn't he,
Helen . . Our Jackie . .

HELEN. He is Granda . .

GEORGE. Another feature of an air raid . . After the planes have
dropped their bombs . . (*Breaks off.*)

JOYCE. What happens, then, Dad . . .

GEORGE. It's torn up . . . Somebody's used what happens next for
wiping themselves on . . .

JOYCE. What else do they do, Eric? . .

ERIC. They machine gun you . .

MAM. Joyce, Helen — come with me . .

JOYCE. Where are you going, Mam . . .

MAM. I want you with us . . The two girls . . . Eric . . I'm sorry . . I
must ask Our Lady something . . . . If I don't . . we'll never get out
of here alive . .

ERIC. I've sealed up the doors, Mrs. Stott . . .

MAM. I must get to me Our Lady . . .

GEORGE. Just use your Rosary, man . . for God's sake . . .

MAM. Will you let me get to Our Lady, for God's sake . . .

HELEN. Mam . . Calm yourself . .

MAM. How can I calm meself when I can't get to Our Lady in me
hour of need . . . Dear God in heaven . . . Will you let me get to
Our Lady!

ERIC. I'm pulling it down, Mrs. Stott . . .

HELEN. (*to* AUDIENCE). And then . . . . It was all our nerves being strung up that did it . . . There was this whine . . . And all of us threw ourselves on the floor . . . Even Granda . . . Then I suddenly realised what the noise was . . . (*She gets up. Goes into the scullery. Returns with the kettle.*) It was the kettle, mam.

MAM. That was your fault, George . . Putting it into people's heads about air raids . . .

ERIC. Better be safe than sorry, Mrs. Stott . . .

They all get up except ANDIE.

ANDIE. Is it all right . . .

HELEN. It was the kettle, Granda . . .

ANDIE. I *thought* it was the kettle . . .

HELEN. Seeing it's boiling . . . I might as well make everybody a cup of tea . . . Will I . . .

JOYCE. You want to see me ring, everybody?

MAM. Yer ring?

HELEN. Your ring?

(*To* AUDIENCE.) God knows when she got it . . . I found out later . . when they were lying on the ground . . . She just said 'yes' to him . . . . So that was how our Joyce got engaged . . . .and how Hitler changed my life too . . .

MAM. Eee . . It's a lovely ring . . Isn't it . . .

GEORGE. Cannie . .

HELEN. It's nice . .

MAM. Eee . . Look at the state of me blankets and pillows . . .

GEORGE. There's a war on, man . . . What's a bit of soot on a pillow . . .

HELEN (*to* AUDIENCE). I was watching our Joyce with Eric . . Sitting at the table . . drinking their tea . . . Joyce not being able to keep her eyes off the ring . . . . shining on her finger . . I just had to think of the song . . the Coalman was playing . . He was sitting at the piano . . with his mug of tea on the top . . . . Playing away . . . .

Oh Johnnie, Oh Johnnie,
How you can love,
Oh Johnnie, Oh Johnnie,

Heavens above,
You make my glad heart jump with joy . . . etc . . .

. . . I can just bring it right back . . the smells and the sight . . and the sound . . and all me feelings . . watching the two of them . . sitting there . .

Oh Johnnie . . etc . . . .

Scene Two

We'll Meet Again . . .
20, 21 June 1940

HELEN (*to* AUDIENCE). The only place he knew in Newcastle was Eldon Square . . There was a bench, under a three . . . He said to meet him in Eldon Square . . . on Sunday afternoon . . . I really thought he was having us on . . I went . . I sat down on the seat . . There was nobody there but me . . . No sign of him . . . . I felt funny sitting there . . Waiting for him . . . . I felt funny going down to Eldon Square . .

It was one of these bad days for my ankle . . . Some days it really got us down . . . I walked worse than ever . . It might've been my nerves . . . I don't know . . . I had on a swagger coat, I'd just bought that week in Parish's . . and turban . . Cost us three and eleven . . me turban . . I looked in the mirror before I went off . . and I looked terrible . . . He was hours late . . . I'd brought the Sun with us . . . Just not to look daft, sitting on me own . . I saw him coming across the Square . . But I kidded on I was reading me Sunday Sun . . .

NORMAN. It's me . .

HELEN. Oh . . So I see . .
(*To* AUDIENCE.) They'd already given him his nickname . . He was the Tailor's Dummy . . . He was always so neat and tidy . . and his face was scrubbed so clean . . I was nearly saying to him: Hullo, Tailor's dummy . . .

NORMAN. What do you fancy doing?

HELEN. *(looking at him).* I like this square . .

NORMAN. Bought you some chocolates . .

HELEN. Where did you manage to get them . . .

NORMAN. . . . You know . . . If you look you can find . . . You mind if I say something to you . . . Eric'll have told you . . I'm a straight forward chap . . . I saw right away . . you were a very honest, straightforward person yourself . .

HELEN *waits for the worst.*

I don't think your turban does you justice . . .

HELEN. I just bought it Thursday . . In Parish's . . .

NORMAN. You don't mind me being straightforward with you . . Do you? . .

HELEN. It doesn't matter what I wear . . . I look horrible . . Anything I put on . . You get one of them Paris dress designers to make us an outfit . . . and I'll still look like something out of a jumble sale . . . It doesn't bother us . . .

NORMAN. That's not true . . I don't believe that . .

HELEN. It *doesn't* bother us . . .

NORMAN. I meant *you* looking like somebody out of a jumble sale . . . What do you think I asked you out for . . . If I didn't think you looked nice . . . Are you angry with me . . because I said I didn't like your turban . . .

HELEN. I don't *think* so . .

NORMAN. Where would you like to go . . Will we go for a coffee . . . I fancy a coffee . . .

HELEN. I'd like to go up to see the Barrage Balloons . . . In the Leazes Park . . I like seeing them . . . I like watching them winding them up and down . . .

NORMAN. *(looking.)* They're up just now . .

HELEN. They might come down later . . for a bit . . .

NORMAN. Yes . . We'll go and have a look at them then . .

HELEN. Sit down . . .

NORMAN. I thought we were going to see that Barrage Balloon . .

HELEN. I just want to sit here for a minute . . . I like sitting here . . .

NORMAN. Call it *our* square . . then . . will we? . . .

HELEN. 'Our'? . . . .
      (*To* AUDIENCE.) See . . . I just didn't know what to say to him . . .
      or how to treat him . . Or anything . . . I felt really funny . . and
      awkward . . and ugly . . . and a mess . . .

NORMAN. I meant the shape of your face . . That turban . .

HELEN. If it bothers you . . I'll take it off . . .

NORMAN. Yes. Take it off . . Will you . . .

      HELEN *takes off the turban.*

HELEN. Is that better? . .

NORMAN. That's smashing . . It is . . . I'm telling you . . It's got a
      lovely shape . . your face . .

HELEN. That's good, then . . .

NORMAN. It has . .

HELEN. All right . . It has . . About the only thing about us that has
      any shape . . .

NORMAN. That's not true . . And you know it . . .

HELEN (*to* AUDIENCE) . . . And he took me hand . . It made us
      really feel funny . . I went red and everything . . . I couldn't take
      it away from him . . . .

      (*To him.*) Will we go up the Leazes, then . . .

NORMAN. Right . . .

HELEN (*to* AUDIENCE). He still held my hand . . . We walked
      awkwardly out of the square towards the park . . I was limping
      really bad . . . Saying to myself . . . That's the last time he's going to
      ask us out with him . . And I'm not bothered anyway . . . . Bloody
      Eric's fault . . . Bringing him back to Walker in the first place . . .
      It was the Ferry week . . The Coalman was playing 'I love to ride a
      ferry' all bloody week . . . . Middle of June . . I was on night shift . .
      At Parsons . . . Dad was, too . . . Labouring at the Neptune Yard . . . .

GEORGE.   I love to ride a ferry,
             Where music is so merry,
             There's a man who plays the concertina,
             On a moonlit upper deck arena . . .
             Where people all are dancing,

> Where couples are romancing,
> Life is like a mandolin,
> Life is like a mandolin,
> Happy, we sing together,
> Happy, we cling together,
> Happy with the ferryboat serenade . . . .

HELEN (*to* AUDIENCE) . . . That first time Norman came into my life. It was one of *those* perfect June days . . . I was sitting out on the step, in the back yard . . . Eric had disappeared to France, after two days honeymoon with Joyce in Walker . . . and we'd never heard from his since . . . I could get nowt out of Joyce . . *How* she felt . . Everybody was sure he was dead . . . The last of them had got out of Dunkirk three weeks back . . . and *still* we hadn't heard from Eric . . . . First thing that happened was the Old Soldier turned up . . . Two weeks early . . from Auntie Marge's . . . With all his luggage . . .

ANDIE. I stood out there . . Listen to us . . George . . . . I stood out there . . *Entranced* with the music . . .

HELEN. Granda . . You're two weeks *early* . .

ANDIE. No use asking me . . if I'm two weeks early . . or two weeks late . .

GEORGE. You're two weeks early . .

ANDIE. There's a war on . . Different routines in wartime . . . . Where's The Saint? . .

GEORGE. I was thinking of putting a mattress in the shelter . . We've got a shelter, now . . . Did you know? . . . . When I'm on nightshift . . . It's the best place . . Nobody disturbs us there . . .

HELEN. Does me Mam know you're coming . . She doesn't Granda . . Does she? . .

GEORGE. She's gone to the Chapel . . There's a new Father . . . Monaghan's gone to be a Chaplain . . Did you hear . . .

ANDIE. I told you, Helen, man . . It's out of me hands . . . . Not for me to reason why . . . They work it out between them . . Where me next pillow is . . George . . You should never have daughters . . Take your whole life over, daughters . . I know . . Ye've got them . . . Don't say you haven't been warned . . .

GEORGE. I told her to take her statue to see the new priest . . . An outing for her Virgin Mary . . . Give her a bit of fresh air . . .

HELEN. What did you fight with Auntie Marge over, *this* time . .

ANDIE. You should tell yer Da' . . never to laugh at what people believe in . . .

GEORGE. Ye're right, Andie . . . I shouldn't . . .

ANDIE. If they believe in it . . . It's true . . .

GEORGE. It is . . .

ANDIE. I wish *I* bloody believed in something . . .

GEORGE. I believe in Churchill . . . You liked that song . . did you? . .

ANDIE. It's a lovely song, George . . . An excellent cherry song . . excellently played . . .

HELEN. She's got it marked on the calendar . . when you're due . . Look . . . June 24th . . Father . . .

ANDIE. You know that, Helen . . I just take my orders . . They say to us: 'Time you moved on to Peggy . . . Pack yer bags . .' I pack my bags and take me cat . . and move on to Peggy . . Mine is not to reason why . .

GEORGE. Quite right. Best way . . . Move in with me in the shelter . . .

ANDIE. Have ye a pan . . I got a bit of fish for Tibbie . . .

HELEN. Granda . . You're not starting cooking stinking cat fish on top of you turning up two weeks too soon . . . You know how she hates the smell of cat fish . .

ANDIE. Look at them . . cod lugs . . Fresh out the North Sea this morning . . A penny . . .

HELEN. Granda . . Your bed's not made or anything, man . . We haven't changed round the room for you . . .

GEORGE. He's sleeping with me in the shelter . .

ANDIE. I don't think I can sleep in the shelter . .

GEORGE. Give you a hot water bottle . . . *(Mimics an air raid warning.)*

ANDIE *is intent on his cat fish.*

GEORGE. It's Peggy . . The old woman . . She's coming now . .

ANDIE. Listen . . . I think I'll lie down . . A bit . . . . Just tell her I'm here, Helen . . Say . . I was a bit tired . .

HELEN (*to* AUDIENCE). And he ran off with his case and Tibbie . . . It was his lucky day, but . . First thing me Mam did, when she came in, was go to the statue of Our Lady in her room . . .

MAM. George . . Helen . . Come and look . . .

HELEN (*to* AUDIENCE). Me Mam was standing at the statue of Our
Lady . . .

MAM. Can you see? . .

GEORGE. I'm looking . . .

HELEN. What do you see, Ma . .

MAM. Can you not see yourself . . . Look at Our Lady . . .

HELEN. The sun's lovely on her . . .

MAM. She's changed her expression . .

GEORGE. I'm away back to me piano . . .

MAM. George, man . . Look at her . . .

GEORGE. (*not interested*). She's changed her expression . . .

MAM. She has. She's smiling . . . Can you not see, Helen?

HELEN. I'm not sure, Mam . . .

MAM. I felt it, at the chapel . . Helen . . . I was standing there,
praying . . . for Eric . . . And I felt meself all glowing . . . And I came
rushing back here . . . And Our Lady's smiling at us . . . Do you not
see, Helen . . .

HELEN. Eee . . I don't know, Mam . . Maybe . .

MAM. I had this lovely warm feeling . . Kneeling there in the church . . .

HELEN (*to* AUDIENCE). Dad was at his piano, again . . Playing that
Vera Lynn song . . . Granda's fish was boiling . . . for his cat . . . .

GEORGE   We'll meet again,
Don't know where,
Don't know when . .

MAM. What's that smell? . .

GEORGE.   But I know we'll meet again,
Some sunny day . . .

MAM. Who's cooking fish, Helen? . .

GEORGE.   Keep smiling through. Just like you always do,
Till the blue skies drive the dark clouds far away . .

MAM. (*at the fish*). . . Where *is* he? When did the Old Soldier come?

HELEN. He's just a few days early, Mam . . .

MAM. Da .! Da .! Where are you, man . .

GEORGE.   So will you please say hello,
           To the folks that I know,
           Tell them I won't be long,

MAM. Da!

GEORGE.   They'll be happy to know, . .

MAM. Da . . .

HELEN. It's all right . . I'll make his bed . . later . .

ANDIE. *(coming in, guilt all over his face)*. What it was . . Peggy . . .

MAM. You're two weeks too early, Da, man . . It's not fair . . I'm glad
     to see you . . But . . . . An agreement's an agreement . . . Margaret's
     to pull her weight along with the rest of us . .

ANDIE. I'm telling you what happened . . This morning . . . . The sun
     was shining . .

GEORGE.   They'll be happy to know that as you saw me go . . I was
           singing this song . .

MAM. George, can you not give that bloody piano a rest!

ANDIE. What I said to myself was . . It just came into me head,
     Peggy . . Listen to this . . . . Eric is alive and safe and well . .

MAM. Ee . . It didn't, Da . . Did it? . .

ANDIE. I'm telling you . . .

HELEN (*to* AUDIENCE). Me Mam looked straight in his eyes . . . .
     Reading him like a book . . .

ANDIE. All right . . . I'm telling you a lie . . . . People tell people lies . . .
     man . . I made a mistake . . I thought it was time I was here . . I
     packed me bags . . And everything . . this morning . . . And when I
     found out I was two weeks too early . . .

     The truth is . . Keep this to yerself . . Peggy . . . I can't help it . .
     man . . You're me favourite daughter . . . .

MAM. Oh . . For God's sake, Da . . .

ANDIE. You are, man . . I can't help it . . It's the truth . . I miss you . .
     The six months I'm at me other daughter's house . . I'm missing
     you . . .

MAM. Come and see the statue of Our Lady . . Da . . .

HELEN (*to* AUDIENCE) . . . They went in to see the statue . . . . The Coalman started up again . . .

GEORGE.   We'll meet again . . Don't know where, don't know when . . . But I know we'll meet again, some sunny day . . .

ANDIE. *(coming back).* . . . Thank God, then . . He's saved . . . Joyce's man . . Eh . . .

HELEN. Granda, man . . Don't be daft, man . . You don't believe that statue's smiling . . .

ANDIE. If she says it is . . it is . . . Anyway . . It doesn't matter . . Nothing matters . . . Does it . . . We're all bits of life, dancing away, till we burn ourselves out . . .

GEORGE. Or bloody Hitler does it for us . . .

HELEN. Ee . . You're a daft old bugger . . aren't you . . (*To* AUDIENCE.) He was at the cooker . . Stirring his cat fish . .

ANDIE. Cannie bit of cod lug that . . . She'll really enjoy that, Tibbie . . . . Smell it . . .

GEORGE. Bloody smell it alright . . . I'm thinking of putting on me bloody gas mask . . .

HELEN (*to* AUDIENCE) . . . Me Mam must have left the front door open in her excitement . . . Because the Coalman was just saying that . . . When the Lost Boy was in the room with this other soldier . . . Standing there . . . It was like a miracle . . It really was . . The way they were suddenly standing there . . .

ERIC. I'm back, then . .

GEORGE. Eric . . Come here, lad . . Give us yer hand . . . Welcome back son . .

ERIC. Where's the lass, then . . ?

HELEN. She's been very worried about you . . Why didn't you write to her . . .

ERIC. Where *is* she, Helen, man? . .

ANDIE. Who's *he*?

ERIC. Him?

NORMAN. I'm Norman . . .

ERIC. He's from Birmingham.

GEORGE. Peggy, man . . Where are you . . The lad's back . . Where are you . . .

ERIC. Just come from Durham . . .

HELEN. Why didn't you let her know you were back . . .

ERIC. I wrote a letter . . And gave it to this tart . . In Southampton . . .

MAM. Ee . . I can't believe it . . Eric, son . . ! Ee . . *Look* at you . . You're back ! . . . Helen . . Are you going to give them a cup of tea . . .

ERIC. Where's the lass? . .

HELEN. I'll go and get her . . . She's at Parsons . . . She's a job . . at the Blade shop . . I'll get her out . . .

MAM. Did you tell him about Our Lady . . .

GEORGE. We told him about Our Lady . . .

MAM. Isn't that a *miracle*, Eric . . .

ERIC. We all got this letter thing to fill in . . To the next of kin . . . I gave it to this tart . . In Southampton . .

MAM. Did you have a terrible time, pet . . . Getting clear of the Germans . . .

NORMAN. We were lucky. We found this shop with tins of beans . . .

ERIC. Eating cold beans all the way to bloody Dunkirk . . . You ever eaten cold beans . . night and day . . Geordie . . ?

MAM. I've got some sausage and dried egg . . . Would you fancy sausage and dried egg . . .

ERIC. Oh . . I brought you a present (*Handing her a packet of soap powder.*)

MAM. Oh, soap powder! That's nice of you . . .

GEORGE. I was just playing that song . . We'll meet again . . Minute you came in . .

ERIC. So you didn't get me letter? . . I gave it to a tart . . .

HELEN. I'm off to get Joyce . . .

ERIC. Tell her I've a present for her . . .

HELEN. I will . . .

GEORGE. Ye brought her soap powder, too . .

MAM. George, man . . .

ERIC. I just saw it in a shop in Durham . . Had this notice in the window . . Soap powder . . .

MAM. Eee . . Our Joyce's face . . Helen . . When she sees Eric . .

HELEN (*to* AUDIENCE). Our Joyce . . When I got her out of Parsons . . . Halfway home . . she got cold feet . .

JOYCE. What's he like, Helen? . . .

HELEN. He's waiting for you, Joyce . .

JOYCE. Helen . . I can't remember what he's like . . . His face . .

HELEN. Look at his photograph in yer bag . . .

JOYCE. I don't know what to *say* to him . . .

HELEN. Joyce, don't be daft, man . . . Come on . . .

JOYCE. Wait on, Helen . . I need a minute or two to get us together . . Is he wearing his uniform . . . He's not going to sleep in our house . . tonight . . is he? . . . What did he say? . .

HELEN. Joyce . . . Come on . . .

JOYCE. He'll want to do it with us . . tonight . . Minute we go to bed . . . I don't mind him . . . Going to the pictures with him . . and that . . But I can't stand it . . when he's all over us . .

HELEN. You'll be alright, Joyce . . When you get together . . . and see him . . . He's got a present for you . . .

JOYCE. What's he brought . . Stockings . . .

HELEN. Brought me Mam soap powder . . .

JOYCE. I've only known him three days . . haven't I . . . If you count it all up . . . You can't blame us . . . I don't know him . . . I've forgotten all about him . . . I know Geoff Howard in the factory ten times better than I know him . . .

HELEN. You'll be alright . . Once you've broken the ice again . .

JOYCE. You keep saying that . . .

HELEN. It's true . .

JOYCE. Eee . . You do some mad things in yer life, don't you? . . . I *married* him . . . Helen . . . Can you imagine that . . . married *him*!

HELEN. Are you coming . . Joyce, man . .

JOYCE. What am I going to say to him . . .

HELEN (*to* AUDIENCE) . . . . The Lost Boy couldn't hear *what* she said to him . . The Coalman was making such a bloody row on the piano . . .

GEORGE.   So will you please say hello,
             To the folks that I know
             Tell them I won't be long . .

JOYCE. Hullo, Eric . . .

ERIC. What do you say? . . .

JOYCE. Hullo . . .

ERIC. I'll come nearer . . .

MAM. George . . . Give that bloody piano a rest . . . Will you . . People want to talk . . (*To* JOYCE.) Are you not going to give him a kiss . .

JOYCE. Yes . . . (*Not kissing him.*)

ERIC. I'm back then . . I gave this letter to a tart . . Did you get it . . .

JOYCE. I didn't get anything . . No . . .

ANDIE. I'd better come back after his leave . . I came two weeks before me time, Joyce . .

ERIC. I've got three days . . .

JOYCE. It's alright . . Granda, man . . Don't move out for us . . . Eric can sleep in his Mam's . . can't you Eric . . .

ERIC. It's away over in Heaton, Joyce, man . . . You don't want us . . on me first leave, back from France, for you to sleep in Walker and me over in Heaton . .

ANDIE. Listen, it's for the war effort . . . I'll go back to yer Auntie Margaret's, Joyce . .

JOYCE. Granda . . I don't *want* you to go back . . . I like you here . . .

HELEN (*to* AUDIENCE) . . . That was news to him . . Joyce never bloody *looked* at him, whenever he was with us . . .

GEORGE. How about a double mattress in the shelter . . with a hot water bottle . . That was what I was thinking of . .

MAM. Don't be daft, George, man . . . What would they be doing in the bloody shelter . .

GEORGE. Bloody more than they'd be doing, with him in Heaton and her in Walker . .

JOYCE. Do you want a cup of tea, Eric . . .

ERIC. Yer Mam's given us one . .

JOYCE. I think *I'll* have one . .

HELEN (*to* AUDIENCE) . . . Joyce went into the scullery to make the tea . . Eric was going to follow her . . She stopped him . .

JOYCE. You'd better stay and talk to me Mam and Da' . . Eric . .

ANDIE. Should I go then . . What do you think I should do . . .

GEORGE. You'll have that poor bloody cat dizzy . . Picking it up and putting it down again . . .

HELEN. I'd better go to the butchers and see if I can get something for tea, Mam . .

MAM. Ee . . You'd better . . That's right . . .

HELEN (*to* AUDIENCE). Anything to get out of that atmosphere . . . . When I got back . . Me Granda was off with his cases and Tibbie . . . Me Mam and Dad had gone off with Norman to Shields Road . . . Norman wanted to buy something for his Dad's birthday or something . . . Joyce was sitting there . . . drinking her tea . . . She'd put on fresh make up . . . But you could see she'd been crying . . . I felt really sorry for her . . . Me heart went right out out to her . . . Then I said to meself . . What for . . What do you feel sorry for her for . . . She's at least got somebody . . . Even if Eric . . Anyway . . What's wrong with Eric . . . .

(*To* JOYCE *and* ERIC.) . . . I got some liver . . .

ERIC. Yes . . I fancy a bit of liver and onions . . .

JOYCE. That's good . . .

HELEN. I'll go and get things ready for the tea, then . . .

JOYCE. I'll help you . . .

HELEN. I don't need any help . . I can peel onions and potatoes without you helping me . . . Sit down and finish your tea . . . .

(*To* AUDIENCE.) I shut meself up in the scullery . . . . From time to time I heard bits of the talk . .

ERIC. Going to give us a kiss . .

JOYCE. Ahuh . .

ERIC. Go on, then . .

JOYCE. (*a peck*). There you are . .

ERIC. That's not a kiss . .

JOYCE. What is it, then . . If it isn't . . .

ERIC. That's a kiss . . .

JOYCE. Ee . . Stop . . Man . . I can't breathe . . .

ERIC. That's more like it, isn't it . . . Did you miss us . . .

JOYCE. Ahuh.

ERIC. I missed you . . I thought about you all the time . .

JOYCE. That's good . . .

ERIC. I bought you a present . . .

JOYCE. Ta . .

ERIC. Want to see it . . .

JOYCE. Ahuh . .

ERIC. Give us a kiss and I'll show you it . .

JOYCE. *Don't* man — somebody'll come in . .

ERIC. It's only Helen in there . . *She's* not bothered . . . Come on . . .

JOYCE. You've been to the pub . . .

ERIC. Just for a couple . . . There you are . . What do you think . .
    (*Holding up a pair of French knickers.*)

JOYCE. Where did you get *them* from . . .

ERIC. Tart gave us them out of gratitude. . No she didn't . . Bought
    them . . in France . . Real French Knickers . . .

JOYCE. Ee . . I couldn't wear *them* . . !

ERIC. Of course you could . . I've been thinking about you in them,
    ever since I got them . . . .

JOYCE. Anyway . . I think they're the wrong size . . .

ERIC . Go in the bedroom and try them on . . . I'll come with you . . .

JOYCE. Don't be daft, man . .

ERIC. Go on . . Joyce . . Let yourself go . . Have a bit of fun . . .

JOYCE. Do you want a cup of tea . . .

ERIC. No . . I don't want a rotten, bastardin', bloody, effing cup of
    bloody tea . . . . Are you not glad to see us back safe and sound . .

JOYCE. Yes . . I'm very glad. I'm relieved . . .

ERIC. That's good . . .

HELEN (*to* AUDIENCE). I was sorry for both of them . . . then . . .
  I stayed in the scullery as long as I could . . to leave them alone . . .
  One time . . . It looked as if it was going to be alright with them . . .

JOYCE. If you just give us a day or so . . Eric . . To get used to you

ERIC. All right . .

Joyce. I'm just a very funny character . . You know that . . . Just
  don't keep pushing us . .

ERIC. Alright . . It's okey dokey . . . You're still my sweetheart, aren't
  you?

JOYCE. Yes.

ERIC. That's alright then . .

    (*To* AUDIENCE.) And they all bloody came back then . .
  The Coalman with a new bit of music . . . He couldn't *wait* to try
  it . . .

  That certain night, The night we met . . There was magic abroad in
  the air . . . etc . . .

HELEN. Norman came into the scullery . . .

NORMAN. Brought you a present . .

HELEN. Me?

  The song continues.

NORMAN. Just some scent . . In Parrish's shop . . .

HELEN. Ta . . That's nice . . . I've never used scent very much . .
  Evening in Paris . . Lovely bottle . . Isn't it . .

NORMAN. Fancy going out some time . . Two of us . . .

HELEN. *Me* . . . ?

NORMAN. I don't need to go back till tomorrow night . . .

HELEN. Where to like . . .

NORMAN. Meet you in the town . . I know Eldon Square . . . You
  know Eldon Square . . Could meet you there . .

HELEN. If you *want* . . .

NORMAN. Do *you* want . . ?

HELEN. I don't mind . . . .

    (*To* AUDIENCE) That bloody song the Coalman was singing . . .

And him looking at us . . . I had this feeling . . Like I was in one of them films . . With all the music playing . . . .

GEORGE.   The moon that lingered over London Town . . etc . . .

HELEN (*to* AUDIENCE). I went into the kitchen . . Joyce and Eric were sitting there . . . Not looking at each other . . The Coalman was singing his bloody heart out . . . Both of them had this really sad look on their faces . . .

GEORGE. Poor puzzled moon . . He wore a frown . . . etc . . .

HELEN. Norman kept looking at me . . Nobody had ever looked at us like that before . . In my whole life . .

Up song.

Scene Three

Yours
12 August 1940

ERIC *and* JOYCE *tangoing* . . . . .

GEORGE.   Yours till the stars lose their glory,
Yours till the birds fail to sing,
Yours to the end of life's story,
This pledge to you dear, I bring.
Your's in the grey of December,
Here or on some far distant shores,
I've never loved anyone the way I love you,
How could I? When I was born to be,
Just your's . . .

. . .   This night has music,
The sweetest music,
It does something with my heart,
I hold you near me,
Oh darling hear me,
I have a message I must impart . . .

ERIC. Come on and dance, Helen . . . Come on . .

JOYCE. Helen doesn't dance, Eric man . . . It's her foot . . .

HELEN I *can't* dance . .

ERIC. Come on . . .

HELEN. I can't . . .

JOYCE. Leave her alone . . .

GEORGE.   Yours till the stars lose their glory, etc . . .

HELEN (*to* AUDIENCE) . . . That was the one thing that got us
about my leg being bad . . . I couldn't dance . . . Ee . . I was really
jealous of Joyce . . the way she could dance with Eric . . . It was the
one thing I was jealous about . . . Lasses being able to dance . . . .

That day . . Anyway . . I couldn't settle on anything . . . I was dying
to get to Eldon Square to see Norman . . If he was coming . . . He
was supposed to be getting twenty four hours leave . . . But with all
the air raids . . we'd heard all the leaves were cancelled . . . Even
Eric was called back to his camp, that day . . . And he was only on
training soldiers . . . This telegram came . . Ee . . My heart was in
my mouth . . . I thought something had happened to Norman . . . .
It was just calling back Eric . . . . He tore it up . . . in the stupid way
he always carried on . .

ERIC. I didn't get that telegram . . . Did you see us get a telegram . . .
Joyce . . . Just bloody got here . . and they're shouting for us to
come back . . .

MAM. Hitler's due, Eric, pet . . Any minute . . .

GEORGE. If we're depending on Eric to stop the bugger, he'll be
arriving at the Central Station, first thing tomorrow morning . . .

MAM. Don't *say* that, George, man . .

JOYCE. Eric . . . Don't be daft . . . . If it says you've to go back . . .
You've to go back . . .

HELEN (*to* AUDIENCE). You could see . . . She was relieved she
hadn't to spend the night with him . . .

ERIC. I've just bloody got here . . .

MAM. I'll make you a scrambled egg and toast and onions . . Have we
got an onion, Helen? . .

HELEN. Got an onion . . .

MAM. And a cheese sandwich for the train . . .

HELEN (*to* AUDIENCE). And then the Old Soldier comes in with all
his gear . . and the cat basket . . and a baby's gas mask . . .

GEORGE. Here he comes . . Britain's Secret Weapon . .

ANDIE. August 14th . . . it's in the papers . . He's arriving in London . . . Adolf . . . Am I right? . . . you not read the papers . . .

GEORGE. *(with the papers).* Wrong . . . August fifteenth . . . It's only the thirteenth today . . So you've two days . . And he'll take another day from London to Newcastle . . .

ANDIE. It's all over . . Bar the shouting . . . Next year, this time, we'll all be singing Deutschland Uber Alles . . and speaking German . . I've always meant to learn a foreign language anyway . . .

JOYCE. Helen . . You speak to him . . He's going to end up behind bars . . . You are . . .

ANDIE. Have you got me ration books, Peggy . . . I'll need me ration books . . .

MAM. Where's he going? Where are you going, man . . .

ANDIE. Not bloody staying here for Hitler to find us . . . I'm going to Wooler . . .

ERIC. He's not coming . . That's defeatist talk, Mr. Ryan . .

GEORGE. If the whole British army's dancing around with their lasses like you, son, I wouldn't be too bloody sure.

ANDIE. I want me ration books, Peggy . . .

MAM. Sid down, you daft old bugger . . I'm making everybody scrambled egg sandwiches . .

ANDIE. That's another thing . . Once I'm in Wooler . . I'll get some real eggs . . Gets on yer nerves that egg powder . . .

ERIC. I just got here, Mr. Ryan . . . It's not right . . Is it . . . Ten minutes after I get here . . They send this telegram . . . . Six months . . man . . Since I've seen me wife . . isn't it . . .

ANDIE. That's up to you . . isn't it . . . To work out if it's worth getting shot for . . .

ERIC. Who's getting shot? . . .

GEORGE. That's right . . King's regulations . . Desertion of post . . .

ANDIE. You get some insects like that . . . Don't you . . . They die, soon as they've mated . . It's worth it to them . . Dying . . For a night of love . . . Can't understand it meself . . Never been worth all that to *me* . . . What about *you* George? . . .

HELEN *(to* AUDIENCE) . . . And just as me Dad was trying to work

that out, the bloody sirens sounded . . . He jumped into action . .
Put on his Warden's helmet . .

GEORGE. Right . . Everybody into the shelter . .

MAM. The shelter's bloody flooded, man . . I'm not going in there . . .
And I'm sure it's a nest of rats . . . I definitely saw a rat there . .

ANDIE *has produced a baby gas mask.*

GEORGE. What's *he* doing? . . What's that you've got . . .

ANDIE. Just something I picked up . . .

GEORGE. Everybody in the shelter . . .

MAM. I don't care if a bomb strikes us down here and now . . . I am not
going into that rat hole . . .

GEORGE. That is a *Baby Respirator* . . . Where did you get it from? . . .

ANDIE. . . . I picked it up . . . It's for Tibbie, man . . .

GEORGE. That's Government property . . That's for *babies* . . .

ANDIE. I'm telling you . . a man got us it . . . For a banjo . . Me old
banjo . . . I gave him . . .

GEORGE. You gave him away that old banjo . . . . *I* wanted that
banjo . . .

ANDIE. I'll get you another one . . .

HELEN (*to* AUDIENCE) . . . . We could hear from the coast . . The
Anti Aircraft guns starting up . . . Me Mam turned white . . .

MAM. Eee . . Dear Jesus . . I'll never see this war out . . . I know
that . . . .

GEORGE. That's Black Market . . . You know that . . You can be
charged on two counts . . . Listen . . I've warned you . . Get into
your air raid shelter . . .

MAM. George . . Where are you going man . . The bombs are falling all
over the place . . .

GEORGE. I'm Block Warden . . Amn't I . . . I've me duty . . .

ANDIE. It was not Black Market . . I am opposed to all black
marketeering . . I gave me banjo for it . .

GEORGE. Two counts . . . In an emergency . . . The authorities have
powers to shoot you for less than that . . . You are robbing some
innocent baby of a respirator . . .

ANDIE. He got *two* . . Chap that sold us it . . . Said he'd lost one . . . I asked him to get hold of one for me cat . . .

GEORGE. Give me that respirator!

ANDIE. What you want us to do . . . Stand by and let me cat be gassed to a slow death . . . Have you ever seen anybody gassed, you stupid bugger . . .

GEORGE. As Block Warden, by virtue of the authority given to me, I order you to give me that respirator . .

ANDIE. Go and have a shit to yerself, Geordie Stott . . .

MAM. They're going to get the church, this time . . I know it . . . Listen to them . . .

HELEN. That's just the guns, Mam . . .

MAM. I know . . . In me heart . . You know how I know them things . . . like I knew Mrs. Wilcox was going to pass away that week . . .

HELEN. She *didn't* pass away, Mam . . .

MAM. She twisted her ankle, didn't she . . . In the blackout . . . That church is going to get it . . . I know . . . And it's *my* fault . . .

GEORGE. Are you going to give me that respirator . . . ?

ERIC. Will I take it from him, Mr. Stott . . .

GEORGE. I'm the Warden here . . . Even soldiers . . . Take orders from the Civil Defence . .

ERIC. Do they? . . .

GEORGE. Right . . Leave it at that . . . I'm not going to fight over it . . . I am reporting you . . .

HELEN (*to* AUDIENCE). I felt really let down . . . I was sure now . . . Norman would never get away from Tynemouth . . . They'd have them all at the battery . . . It was just like . . . the whole day collapsed round us . . . That had never happened to us before . . Planning a day on somebody else . . Seeing somebody . . . I mean . . . We'd just go to the Leazes Park and watch the ducks . . . and go to the Balloon Barrage and talk . . .

GEORGE. I'm taking down your name . . .

ANDIE. Shouldn't ye be getting to your post . . ?

ERIC. You not think we might be better in the shelter . . Mrs. Stott . . .

MAM. Eee . . I don't know where we should be son . . God only knows . .

JOYCE. Maybe . . If you prayed to Our Lady . . Mam . . .

MAM. Ee . . I *can't* man . . That's the trouble . . . I can't look her in the eyes . . .

JOYCE. Mam . . What's the matter . . .

MAM. Don't *ask* . . . Joyce . . . Don't ask . . . I can't tell you . .

JOYCE. Helen . . Our Mam's upset . . . Look at her . . .

HELEN. What's the matter, Mam . . .

MAM. I don't know what's the matter . . . Are you making the egg . . .

ERIC. If we're not going to the shelter . . I wouldn't mind a sandwich . . .

MAM. Eee . . I don't know where I am . . . Make him a sandwich . . .

ANDIE. Get to yer post, man . . .

GEORGE. I'm putting down your particulars . . . Put down this address . . .

ANDIE. Put where the hell you like . . . I'll be in Wooler . . Before you can do anything about it . . .

GEORGE. You're not taking that gas mask to Wooler . . . It was in the papers this morning . . . A woman got two years for feeding bread to the sparrows.

ANDIE. I'm not feeding bloody sparrows . . . I'm protecting cats from poison gas, man . .

HELEN (*to* AUDIENCE) . . . Then the planes started coming over . . .

MAM. Where are you going, man?

GEORGE. I've got my responsibilities, Peggy . . . I'm Block Warden . . .

MAM. I don't want you to go out . . . I've got a feeling . . . Will you listen to us . . . .

ANDIE. It doesn't matter . . Peggy, man . . . what happens . . . nothing matters . . . . In the end . . . All that's left's the grass . . Isn't it . . . That's all . . . That's what I'm saying . . . It's not worth getting all that worked up about . . .

ERIC. This air raid . . Could last for hours . . Couldn't it . . . I'll say I missed my train . . .

MAM. Ee . . That's a bomb . . Isn't it . . George . . Is that a bomb . . . ?

JOYCE. You said you were up for stripes . . Eric . . . . . If you start going about disobeying orders . .

ERIC. You not want us to stay tonight?

JOYCE. Yes . . I want you to stay tonight, Eric . . What do you think . . .

ERIC. What are you arguing about then . . .

ANDIE. She doesn't want you shot for deserting your post . . .

ERIC. I'm not deserting . . am I . . . I'm just having one night's decent sleep in a decent bed . . . with my wife . . .

JOYCE. Getting into all that trouble . . For one night . . .

ERIC. You not miss us when I'm away . . . When I'm away? . .

JOYCE. Yes . . . I miss you . . . Da' . . stop pushing us . .

GEORGE. I've got to get to my post, Joyce, man . .

HELEN (*to* AUDIENCE). In the end . . . A bomb fell really near us and we all ran for the shelter . . . Granda . . leading with his cat basket . . .

GEORGE. Have you got to bring that bloody cat with you . . . Hurry up, man . . .

MAM. Look at it . . . It's up to your ankles . . .

GEORGE. I've brought me wellies . . Put me wellies on . . .

MAM. Eee . . I hate that miserable shelter . . .

GEORGE. Did you bring a candle . . Helen . . . Where's a candle . . .

HELEN. I've got a candle . .

ERIC. If you're not bothered . . Me staying tonight . . I was doing it for you . . . All right . . Okey dokey . . . I'll go off . . soon as the All Clear's here . . . I'll go now . .

JOYCE. Eric . . Stop fighting with us . . . There are more important things to worry about just now . . .

GEORGE. Right . . . I'll be back soon as I can . . .

MAM. No . . . *(holding him.)*

GEORGE. Let go of us . . . Helen . . man . . Tell her . . I've got to go to my post, Peggy . . . You knew that . . when I signed up to be a Warden . . . I've got my duties . . .

MAM. Yer first duties yer wife and children . . .

ANDIE *makes to go.*

MAM. Where are you going, *now*, Da' . . .

ANDIE. I've left her gas mask . . Tibbie's gas mask . .

ERIC. They're not gassing today, Mr. Ryan . .

ANDIE. I'm taking no chances, son . .

GEORGIE. Will you stay put . . . Bloody shrapnel's flying all over the place . . .

ANDIE. Give us yer tin hat . . then . . Till I get the mask . .

HELEN. *I'll* get it, Granda . . . I'll make a flask of tea for people . . .

MAM. Helen . . Will *you* stay put . . .

GEORGE. Nobody is leaving this shelter . . .

HELEN. Let me get him the mask, Da . . . And I'll make some tea . . .

GEORGE. I've got to get to my post . . .

MAM. I don't want any tea . . .

ERIC. I wouldn't mind a cup of tea . . .

Bomb.

MAM. Listen to that . . .

ANDIE. I want that *mask* . . Ye bugger!

GEORGE. Right . . I'll *get* yer bloody mask!

ANDIE. You're a gentleman, George . . .

ERIC. Soon as the All Clear's come, I'll go . . . You think I'd better go, Mrs. Stott . .

MAM. Ee . . . It's no use asking me . . . My nerves are up to high Doh, pet . . . I don't know what anybody should do . . .

JOYCE. *Go* back in the *morning*, then . . . If you have to . . .

MAM. Joyce . . will you stop fighting . . . I can't stand it . . On top of everything else . . .

GEORGE. There's yer bloody mask . . . But ye're not taking it to Wooler . . .

ANDIE. I've got yer mask, pet . . Don't worry . . Ye'll be alright . . . I know he doesn't understand a bloody word . . But I *do* . .

GEORGE. Can I go to my post now . .

MAM. No . .

HELEN (*to* AUDIENCE). Then the planes were on top of us . . A wave of them . . . The whole shelter was like vibrating with the noise of them . . . Me Mam was moving her lips . . . You could read her praying . . Her eyes shut . . Saying the same words over and over again . . . Into herself . . . Then the bombs began to drop . . . At first away from us . . Then closer . . .

MAM. They've got the church . . I know it . . George . . That was the church . . . They've got . . . I know . . .

GEORGE. Nowhere near the church . . . Take it easy lass . . .

MAM. *Nothing* is safe . . . Even the house of God . . . What am I going to do, Helen . . What am I going to do, for God's sake . . .

HELEN. Mam . . . It's alright . . It'll be alright, Mam . . .

Bombs.

MAM. You don't know the half of it . . It's me . . . It's all *my* fault . . .

ANDIE. If that's all your fault . . Peggy, man . . All I can say is . . I never knew you had it *in* you . . .

HELEN. Granda . . shut up a minute . . .

GEORGE. Here . . I brought some lemonade . . . Give her a sip of lemonade . . .

ERIC. Christ . . . That was a near one . . .

MAM. I know . . . . . They've laid it flat . . . The whole church . . . Everything's been destroyed . . . Father Kennelly's and the other fathers . . .

GEORGE. Will I go and see . . .

MAM. Stay here . . . For God's sake . . .

GEORGE. It's quietening down a bit . . .

ERIC. I'd go . . But I haven't me steel helmet with us . . . And there's all that shrapnel . . .

MAM. George . . Lend Eric your helmet . . .

GEORGE. Let *me* go, man . .

HELEN. Stay here, Da . . She's upset . . .

JOYCE. Will I come with you . . ?

ERIC. Don't be daft, Joyce . . What do you want to come with me for . . .

MAM. You're wasting your time, Eric . . I know . . . It's down . . I know . . .

GEORGE *pulls out his mouth organ and plays 'Hang Out The Washing'.*

ANDIE. Tell ye what . . Give us the Last Post . . .

JOYCE. Granda . . For God's sake . . .

ANDIE. I like it on the mouth organ . . Yer Da' plays it beautiful . . Somebody's bound to have had their number up them bombs dropping . . .

GEORGE. Here's a good one . . You like this one Andie . . . You are my sunshine, My only sunshine . . .

ANDIE. That's a good one . . . (*Joining in.*)

GEORGE.   . . . The other night dear,
            As I lay dreaming . . . (*Breaks off.*)

What the hell's that smell . .

ANDIE. What smell . .

JOYCE. God . . They're not dropping gas . . . And Eric's out there . . .

ANDIE. He's got his mask . . .

GEORGE. Not bloody gas . . .

MAM. I can't smell anything . . . I'm too upset . . .

GEORGE *sniffing, traces the smell to the cat.*

GEORGE. It's that bloody moggie . . He's shit himself in his basket . . .

JOYCE. He has . . . It's horrible . . .

MAM. Get it out of here . . Will you . . . Dad . . .

ANDIE. It's a natural thing . . . I don't know what you're all making such a song and dance over it for . . Happens to everybody . . everybody shits . .

GEORGE. Not in bloody cat baskets. . .

ANDIE. What else can he do . . . You want us to fit it out with a flush lavatory . . . ?

GEORGE. Just get him out, man . . .

ANDIE. In that . . .

HELEN (*to* AUDIENCE). There was just going to be another fight . . .
About throwing out Tibbie . . when the All Clear sounded . . . .
Eee . . I was so happy . . . I could go down to see if Norman was
coming . . . . Even if he wasn't . . Just going down to Eldon
Square . . sitting on our seat . . . . Me Mam came into us . . When I
was in the kitchen . . . She shut the door behind her . .

MAM. Listen, Helen . . On Sunday . . After Mass . . Father Kennelly . .
You know how they stand at the door . . as you go out . . He said to
us: He couldn't help seeing us saying the Lord's Prayer . . . You
could see . . He'd never seen anybody say it like that before . . . Like
I believed in it with my whole body and soul . . .

HELEN. You do, Mam . . .

MAM. I haven't finished, yet, man . . He touched us . . the back of my
hand . . . Standing there in his lovely priest's vestments . . You know
what I mean . . And the light through the glass windows . . That
picture of Jesus . . The light was coming through the windows . . .
Shining on his face . . . He touched my hand . . It gave us a funny
feeling . . You know what I mean . . . You probably wouldn't . .
Joyce would . . But I couldn't tell Joyce . . . I don't want Joyce to
hear this . . . You listening to me Helen . .

HELEN. I *know* what you mean, Mam . .

MAM. It was a real sinful thought . . . The feeling was sinful . . . And I
never told him at Confession . . . How could I? . . It was him that
was in the Confessional . . Father Kennelly . . . But that feeling . .
It was like sometimes when you hear a choir and an organ bursting
into a lovely hymn . . . Or you go in the park . . on a lovely summer
day . . . It made us really feel glad to be living . . . Looking at his
face . . and knowing there was such a person in the world . . .

HELEN. That's not sinful, Mam . . . Don't be daft . . That's lovely . . .

MAM. It is, Helen, man . . . You don't know the half of it . .

HELEN. It isn't . . It's lovely . . . It is . . . You're a daft bloody soul . . .
But some of the things you come out with . . . They're lovely . . .

MAM. I'll help you with the supper . . .

HELEN (*to* AUDIENCE). Then Eric came back . . with Joyce . . .
She'd gone out to look for him . . Frightened he'd been hit by a
bomb or something . . They came back . . . Looking a bit more
together . . .

ERIC. Yes . . I might as well stay . . I got on the 'phone to the station . .
The train I'd have to get . . . I'd miss my supper . . .

MAM. What about the church . . God . . I forgot all about it for the minute . . . *(Going to the window.)*

ERIC. It's alright . . Mrs. Stott . . . Some shrapnel's gone through the roof . . and a couple of windows have been blown in with the blast . . .

MAM. Thank God . . Dear God . . Thank God . . . for saving us, this day . . Amen . . . It's not the one with Jesus in the Cross . . .

ERIC. I never noticed, Mrs. Stott . . .

MAM. Just two windows . . ?

ERIC. Two or three . . .

MAM *(to HELEN)*. There you are . . You see . . That's me being warned . . .

JOYCE. About what, Mam? . . .

MAM. Just been warned . . that's all . . By God . . .

GEORGE.   Yours till the stars lose their glory . .

MAM. Get away, man . . I'm trying to make the supper . . .

GEORGE.   Yours till the birds fail to sing . . . etc . . .

ERIC *and* JOYCE *tangoing.*

HELEN *(to AUDIENCE)*. I couldn't stand watching them any longer . . I got me coat . . and ran off to Eldon Square . .

MAM. Helen, pet . . You haven't had anything to eat . .

HELEN *(to AUDIENCE)*. He was there . . Waiting for us on our seat . . . But he was huddled up . . . Not moving . . . I thought maybe he'd been there since the raid . . and some shrapnel had hit him or something . . .

HELEN. *(Shaking him gently)* . . Norman . . . Are you alright . . . Norman . .

NORMAN. All Clear . . .

HELEN. For hours . . .

NORMAN. I've got twenty four hours leave . . . Been up five nights running . . . They gave me twenty four hours leave . . .

HELEN. You should've come up to the house . . . If you were tired . . .

NORMAN. I like meeting you here . . I'm alright, now . . . Just settled in with a sandwich and a lemonade . . and the siren started . . Couldn't budge . . . I was finished . . .

HELEN. Will I take you home for a rest? . . .

NORMAN. I've twenty four hours leave . . First twenty four hours
    we've got together . . isn't it . . . We've got a whole twenty four
    hours . . . I know . . . Could've been . . . I put my helmet on . .

HELEN. You look a bit daft in it . . . Take it off . . .

NORMAN. What are we going to do . .

HELEN. If I 'phoned them . . I could maybe get tomorrow off . . . I
    could work extra time Thursday and Friday . . .

NORMAN. You look nice . . .

HELEN. Don't be daft, Norman . . .

NORMAN. You *do* . . . Do you always have your hair pinned up . . ?

HELEN. It's easier . . It gets in a mess . . . if I let it loose . . .

NORMAN. Let's see . . .

HELEN. Don't be daft, man . . People are watching . . .

NORMAN. Nobody's watching . . . Nobody here . .

HELEN. We could go to the pictures . . You like Charlie Chan . . .
    Charlie Chan's on at the Welbeck . . .

NORMAN. Go on . . Let it down . . I'm telling you . . I know . . It'll
    suit you . .

HELEN. It'll just be a mess . . I know . . There you are . . I told you . .

NORMAN. It's lovely . .

HELEN. You don't need to say these things to us, Norman . . I keep
    telling you that . . .

NORMAN. It's lovely . . . Your hair's really lovely . . .

HELEN. Will we go up to the Leazes . . .

NORMAN. Listen . . . Let's go daft . . eh . . Come on . . . I feel like
    it . . . I want to go to the Oxford . . . Tonight . . With you . . .

HELEN. Norman . . man . . . . That upsets us . . . Don't keep pulling us
    to dances . . . . I hate that . . .

NORMAN. I want to dance with you . . . What's the matter with your
    leg, anyway . . . It looks alright to *me* . . . Sometimes, you can
    hardly notice you limping . . . can you?

HELEN. Something to do with one leg being shorter than the other . . .
    They noticed it too late for us to get an operation . . . It doesn't
    bother me . .

NORMAN. A waltz you could do easy . . . I can see . . the way you walk . . . We'll just do the slow dances . . .

HELEN. Norman . . I couldn't, man . . Honest . . I wish you wouldn't talk about it . . .

NORMAN. It is . . Your hair's lovely like that . . .

HELEN (to AUDIENCE). He was making us feel funny . . . The way he was looking at us . . . I couldn't believe it . . I'd get a lad like him . .

NORMAN. Tell you something . . I think I'm really falling for you . . . Do you know that . .

HELEN. You're just trying to get round us . . Will we go over to the park . . .

NORMAN. I promise . . If you hate it . . after the first ten minutes . . . We'll go out . . . Just try it with us . .

HELEN. Why have you got to dance with us . . . I don't understand you Norman . . .

NORMAN. I want to take you to a dance . . That's all . . . It's like faith healing . . You know? . . I'm making your leg better . . .

HELEN. That's a good idea . . .

(To AUDIENCE) . . . . And he puts his arms round us . . . I could smell the soap on his skin . . One of his brass buttons dug into my neck . . But he was lovely . . . The way he kissed us . .

(To NORMAN.) . . How does that cure my leg, then, Norman . . ?

NORMAN. Faith . . . I told you . . Look you're walking better . . Look . .

HELEN. I'm not . . . I don't feel it . . . Am I? . .

(To AUDIENCE.) Ee . . he had me as daft as himself . .

Up Dance Band.

That certain night, the night we met,
There was magic abroad in the air,
There were angels dining at the Ritz . . .
And . . .

NORMAN. . . . A nightingale sang in Eldon Square . .

HELEN (to NORMAN). Ten minutes . . And if I hate it by then . . . I'm going home . .

NORMAN. It's one, two, three . . One together . . Left together . . Right together . . It's easy . . . A waltz . .

HELEN. I know a waltz . . I've watched our Joyce doing it enough
    times . . . Come on, then . . . Let's get it over with . . . If I stand on
    your feet . . Don't blame us . .

NORMAN. That's not a waltz . . It's a slow foxtrot . .

HELEN. I've watched Joyce doing that, too . . .

Up Band.

> I may be right and I may be wrong,
> But I'm certainly willing to swear . .
> There were angels dining at the Ritz,
> And a nightingale sang . . .

NORMAN.   . . . In Eldon Square . .

HELEN. See what I mean . . I'm useless . .

NORMAN. You're dancing . . Look at you . . .

HELEN. I can keep time with the music . . . That's easy enough . . .
    But look at us . . .

NORMAN. Helen, love . . You're dancing . . Look at you . . . You are . . .

HELEN. I'm not . . I'm just moving with the music . . . I'm not
    properly dancing . . .

NORMAN. You are, Helen . . . You dance fantastically . . . Honest . . .
    I don't say things to you . . You know that . .

HELEN. It's just that sherry . . . It's got us so I don't know where I
    am . . Norman . . .

NORMAN. That's the secret then . . . Every time we go to a dance . . .
    we'll fill you up first . . . .

HELEN. You think I *am* dancing?

BAND.   When dawn came stealing up, all gold and blue,
    To interrupt our rendezvous,
    I still remember how you smiled and said,
    Was that a dream or was it true,
    Our homeward step was just as light,
    As the tap-dancing feet of Astaire,
    And like an echo — far away . . .

NORMAN & HELEN.
    A nightingale sang . .
    Its voice really rang . . .
    A nightingale sang . .
    In Eldon Square . . .

HELEN (*to* AUDIENCE). Eee . . We stayed right to the end . . . I'd never been so happy in my life . . . I suppose I wasn't dancing properly . . And my ankle began to hurt a bit . . But just the whole crowd . . Being together . . Moving with everybody in the whole crowd . . . And that last waltz . . .

Up Last Waltz.

. . . Just dancing it, it came to us . . (*to* NORMAN). Norman . . Have you somewhere to stay tonight?

NORMAN. I'm staying with you . .

HELEN. You see Eric's back . . . Otherwise you could've come back to our house . . . Where are you going to go . . ?

NORMAN. I love you . . Do you know that? . .

HELEN. I've no idea why . . .

NORMAN. I've got twenty four hours . . I don't want us to be separated . .

HELEN. I'll be sleeping with me Granda in the same room tonight . . When Eric's home . .

NORMAN. One of the lads . . Says there's hotels . . In Jesmond . . Always got rooms . .

HELEN (*to* AUDIENCE). . . We ended up at this Private Hotel off Osborne Road . . . It had a Vacancies notice outside . .

(*To* NORMAN). There you are . . You'll be all right here . . I'll come over in the morning for you . . .

NORMAN. Helen . . I don't want you to leave me, love . .

HELEN (*to* AUDIENCE). I couldn't stand leaving him either . . .

(*To* NORMAN.) I've got to get back to Walker, Norman . .

NORMAN. You can't go away from me now . . . How can you do that . . . I've only got twenty four hours . . .

HELEN. I'll come over and have breakfast with you . . .

NORMAN. I don't mean you to stay in the same room with me . . . If we got rooms next to each other . . . That would be good . . . Just under the same roof . . .

HELEN. Norman . . You're daft . . . That sherry's still affecting you . . .

NORMAN. Come on . . It looks a nice clean place . .

HELEN (*to* AUDIENCE). . . You see . . What it was . . I really trusted

him . . He was a really good person . . . It was the first time I felt I could give myself to somebody else like that . . Trusting him . . .

(*To* NORMAN.) . . Me Mam's waiting for us, Norman . . . If I didn't come home . .

NORMAN. Where are you going? . .

HELEN. Let go of us, Norman . . will you . .

NORMAN. I told you, you could dance . . .

HELEN (*to* AUDIENCE). We must've been talking louder than we thought . . Because the wife from the hotel opened the door and asked us what we wanted . . . I have no idea, to this day, what came over us . . Because I just said:
. . . We want a room for tonight . . . A double room . . . Yes we're married . . . The wife looked at us . . And said something like 'That's up to you' . . . Norman couldn't say anything . . . He was so surprised . . . We just signed the book . . . And went upstairs . . . The wife said she could maybe give us a spam sandwich and a cup of tea . . . I was really starving . . . We had it in our room . . . It was nice . . Nice chintzy curtains and matching bed cover . . .

NORMAN. I didn't mean you to come in the same room . .

HELEN. I know that . . . It's a lovely room, isn't it . . Clean and fresh . . .

NORMAN. She's put a hot water bottle in the bed . . . Bit dry — the sandwiches . .

HELEN. They're alright . . . I phoned me Dad's Warden Post . . They're going to tell him . . .

NORMAN. I wasn't trying anything on . . . You know that, Helen, love . . .

HELEN. I know, Norman . . .

NORMAN. But I love you . . .

HELEN. I love you . . .

NORMAN. Will I sleep on the chair then . .

HELEN. If you want . .

NORMAN. I don't mind . .

HELEN. Don't be daft, man . . (*Taking his hand and kissing him.*) . . . I trust you . . You trust me . . We trust each other don't we . . .

(*To* AUDIENCE). . . . I didn't even have a nightie with us . . I had
to go to bed in my petticoat . . . It was a good job I'd borrowed
Joyce's . . . It was a nice yellow one . . . And we didn't do
anything . . in the night . . or the morning . . . We kissed and cuddled
a bit and went to sleep with our arms round one another . . . It was
lovely . . . Having his arms round us . . . Going to sleep . . . and waking
up . . . with him beside us . . . And the sun shining through the
curtains . . .

Bring up 'Yours'.

> Yours to the end of life's story,
> This pledge to you dear, I bring,
> Yours in the grey of December,
> Here or on far distant shores,
> I've never loved anyone the way I love you,
> How could I,
> When I was born to be
> Just yours . . .

Lights fade.

End of Act One

Act Two

Scene One

The Lovely Weekend
November 1942

GEORGE.   I haven't said thanks for that lovely weekend,
           Those two days of heaven you helped me to spend,
           The thrill of your kiss as you stepped off the train,
           The smile in your eyes like the sun after rain.

JOYCE.   To mark the occasion, we went out to dine,
           Remember the laughter, the music, the wine,
           That drive in the taxi, when midnight had flown,
           Then breakfast next morning, just we two alone . .

GEORGE.   You had to go, the time was so short,
           We both had so much to say,

JOYCE.   Your kit to be packed, the train to be caught,
           Sorry I cried but I just felt that way.
           And now you have gone, dear, this letter I pen,
           My heart travels with you, till we meet again,
           Keep smiling my darling,
           And some day we'll spend,
           A lifetime as sweet as that lovely weekend . . .

HELEN.   *(with her rosary).*
           . . Hail Mary, holy Queen, Mother of Mercy,
           Hail our life our sweetness and our hope,
           To thee do we cry, poor banished children of Eve,
           To thee do we send up our sighs,
           Mourning and weeping in this vale of tears.
           Turn then, most gracious advocate,
           Thine eyes of mercy towards us,

And after this, our exile,
Show unto us the blessed fruit of thy womb, Jesus.
Oh clement, oh loving, oh sweet Virgin . . .
Pray for us, oh holy mother of God,
That we may be made worthy of the promises of Christ.

(*To* AUDIENCE.) . . . The week me Mam went to London . . . for her Auntie's funeral . . . I stopped going to Mass . . . I still said my rosary . . . I always felt better after saying it . . . I'd given up going to Confession, months ago . . . I had to confess to adultery with Norman . . . and I didn't believe I *was* committing adultery . . . I wasn't . . . But the whole thing blew up that weekend . . . Me Mam came back from London . . . The Coalman was organising a party . . . He was always having parties . . . from then on . . . Everything began to turn . . . Rommell had been beaten in Africa . . . and papers were all full of it . . . Pictures of Monty . . . and the tanks in the desert . . . Me Dad was in trouble, too, with me Mam . . That was the week he'd joined the Communist Party . . . At the yard . . .

It started with us finding this flat . . . For Norman and me . . . In Elswick . . Clifton Road . . .

NORMAN. It's nice . . I like it . . .

HELEN. Norman, love . . I don't want you to feel I'm pushing you or anything . . Do you hear me . .

NORMAN. I know, Helen . . .

HELEN. I'm not pushing you to marry us or anything, Norman . . . I mean that . . . I'm just sick of having nowhere of our own . . . It'd be lovely . . wouldn't it . . Having a weekend together in our own place . .

NORMAN. Helen . . Look . . . I'm sorry . . . I love you . . .

HELEN (*to* AUDIENCE). When he came out with it at last . . . I felt that I'd known all the time . . I wasn't angry with him . . . I could understand how he hadn't been able to tell me . . . It wasn't *his* fault, anyway . . . It was me pushing him . . .

NORMAN. I mean . . I was just a kid . . when I married her . . .

HELEN. It's all right, Norman . . Honest . . .

NORMAN. I love *you* . . I bloody hate that . . . Hurting you like this . . I couldn't help it . . .

HELEN. It's alright, love . . Only thing that gets us . . Is you spending your leaves with her . . That's all . . . It's understandable . .

NORMAN. I'll spend the next one with you, Helen . . I mean . . If
there's a next one for us to spend together . . . I mean . . . If you
don't finish with us . . .

HELEN. Norman . . Why should I finish with you . . . I love you . . .

NORMAN. What are we going to do?

HELEN. I bought some Ginger Beer and Pasties . . . To see what it felt
like . . . Eating in our own house . . .

NORMAN. I tried . . you know . . Dozens of times . . To tell you . . .
Just stuck in my throat . . .

HELEN. You've told us now . . . Do you want a pasty . . . ?

NORMAN. Bloody hated it . . You know . . Telling you lies . .

HELEN. I know you did . . Will I scratch your eyes out or something . .
To make you feel better . . Put your coat down . . .

(*To* AUDIENCE.) . . We sat on his greatcoat on the floor . . . It was
a cold November afternoon . . . But the sun was out . . . Coming
through the windows . . .

(*To* NORMAN.) . . I got a lipstick in Parish's . . 'Evening in Paris' . . .
3/8d. it cost us . . . You like it . . ?

NORMAN. I mean . . . I was nineteen . . so was she . . . When we got
married . . .

HELEN. I'll tell you one thing, Norman . . If you really don't want me
to kick in your teeth, love . . I don't really want to hear any more
about you and her . . Just now . . . I know all I want to know . . .
now.

Up 'The Cossack Patrol'. GEORGE *singing it.*

HELEN (*to* AUDIENCE). . . Eee . . My poor Mam . . She came back
full of it . . From the joys of London . . And found her whole world
collapsing round her . . .

JOYCE. Helen . . Come in me room a minute . . I want to talk to
you . . .

GEORGE. Wait a minute, man . . She hasn't had a drink yet . . . What's
his name hasn't had a drink yet . . . What are you going to drink,
Comrade . . .

HELEN. What's happened to me Mam, Da . . .

ANDIE. She's been kidnapped by the German High Command . . .

HELEN. Where's me Mam . .

JOYCE. Helen . . I want to talk to you . . .

GEORGE. I went to the station . . . Three hours late . . The train from London . . I'll go back in an hour . . We'll all go back . . . The Old Soldier's getting married again . . Has he told you . . .

(*To* NORMAN — *with books*.) . . There you are, then . . . You take them back to your camp, son . . Hand them round the other lads . . . If you want . . I'll send somebody over to sign you all on . . . Could you *get* a better system, son . . 'From each according to their ability, to each according to their need.' . . .

ANDIE. Beautiful words . . Only thing to touch it's the Sermon on the Mount . . .

GEORGE. Talking about *real* politics now, Andy, man . . Not your opium of the masses.

Listen . . What will I give you for a wedding present . . I'll play the organ for you . . will I? . .

ANDIE. I'll let you be Godfather at me first christening, son . . .

HELEN. Granda . . You're not getting married, are you . . Eee . . He's not . . .

JOYCE. He's just answered an advert in the Chronicle about a woman with a spare room . . . That's all . . .

ANDIE. Sixty-eight . . . Deaf . . . Wants a bit of company . . . Frightened of the air raids . . . Five bob a week . . . I'm getting bloody sick of getting pushed from pillar to post every bloody day . . . It's upsetting Tibbie . . . She needs a settled home . . doesn't she . .

JOYCE. Are you coming to help us with the sandwiches? . .

HELEN (*to* AUDIENCE). Into the scullery into more problems . . .

JOYCE. I'm bloody pregnant . . Helen . .

HELEN. That's nice . . I'm really happy . . .

JOYCE. For Christ's sake . .

HELEN. Do you not want to be . .

JOYCE. What do *you* think . . . I don't know whose it is . . Helen, man . . .

HELEN. It's Eric's . . .

JOYCE. I'm trying to work out . . when Eric was last on leave . . Was it the last leave . . He only came for the day . . ?

HELEN. Was there all that many . . You can't work it out . . .

JOYCE. If Eric stayed the night his last leave, I'm alright. One of his last two leaves . . he just spent the day here, remember?

HELEN. I'm trying to think on . .

JOYCE. It was an Air Force lad . . Ian . . He was really cannie . . from Scotland. We just fell into it. That was the first time . . . . I'll tell you something . . . I don't know how it was but it's the first time I've enjoyed myself with a lad.

HELEN. Did you not use protection . . .

JOYCE. We just fell into it . . I'm telling you . . . Eee . . What can I do, Helen . . . Can I get rid of it? . . .

HELEN (to AUDIENCE). . . . And then me Mam came in . . Full of it . . . a load of parcels in her arms . . . In her funeral costume . . .

MAM (to GEORGE). Where were you, man? . . . I'll talk to you, after . . Ee . . Helen . . Joyce . . The time I've had . . . I'll show you what I've got . . . Hullo Norman . . .

GEORGE. I stood in that bloody freezing station . . over an hour, Peggy . .

MAM. After bringing you a present . . I went all over London looking for something nice for you . . .

GEORGE. Did she leave you anything? . .

MAM. I didn't go for her to leave me anything . . I went to pay respects to me Da's sister . . . They were asking for you Da' . . Everybody . . .

GEORGE. He's too busy . . . Getting married . . .

MAM. Eee . . He's not . . . Da . .

GEORGE. What did she leave you . .

MAM. She left me Da her piano . .

ANDIE. That's nice of her . . Bring it with you . . Did you?

MAM. Eee . . You should've seen me and yer Auntie Marge . . . In this Rolls Royce . . Going to the funeral . . . Joyce . . . You know what your Auntie Marge is like when she's had a sherry . . . She was putting her hand out the window . . Like the Queen . . Waving, to the crowds . . . Look at this cake . . The shops are full of them . . .

HELEN (to AUDIENCE). She started emptying her bag . . Full of all kinds of rubbish . . It was a shame for her . . . The cream cake . . had

that artificial cream in it . . Like Zinc Ointment . . . And she'd
bought some pies . . and they'd turned in the train . . . The only
decent thing she'd bought was some material . . .

MAM. The black market there . . All over the place . . . What do you
think of that . . . There's a dress length for you and Joyce there . .
isn't there, Helen . . .

JOYCE. Mam . . We can't wear the same dress, man . . Can we . . ?

MAM. *I'll* wear it then . . There's yer present, George . . . I got you
some tobacco . . for making cigarettes, Da . . It's somewhere . . .
I've got a London paper, Norman. Would you like to look at it . . .

NORMAN. Thanks Mrs. Stott . . .

GEORGE. There's yer sherry, Peggy, man . .

MAM. I don't want sherry, at this time of day . . .

GEORGE. It's a party . . . Celebrating Tobruk . . and you getting safe
back from the battlefield . . . Prosit!

JOYCE. Mam . . Do you remember when Eric was last home on leave . . .
For the day — was it last time or the time before . . ?

MAM. The mistake was to let your Auntie Marge take anything before
the funeral . . . You should've seen her at the cemetery . . . I didn't
know where to look . . . She had a fit of the giggles . . . just as they
were laying the poor soul to rest . . . Eee . . The policeman . . There
was this lovely policeman . . Six foot tall . . . We got lost near
Trafalgar Square.

GEORGE. Peggy . . . I might as well tell you this straight away . . .

MAM. It really upset us . . You not being there at the station . . . It was
a let-down . . Bob was there . .

GEORGE. Bloody would be . .

ANDIE. This isn't meant as an offence to you, Peggy . . . But I saw this
in the Chronicle . . Room offered for reasonable charge . . .

GEORGE. I'm bloody trying to tell her something . .

HELEN (*to* AUDIENCE). Then me Mam noticed Norman with all
them Communist papers . .

MAM. Did *you* bring them into this house, Norman?

JOYCE. When did our Eric come home on leave, Mam . . For the day?

ANDIE. So I went up . . Just out of curiosity . . It's in Heaton . . . Just
beside the library . . and the park . . .

MAM. Norman . . You know the Communists do not believe in God . . Them's Communist papers . . . Do you know that . . . Anti-Christ . .

HELEN. They're not his, Mam . . .

JOYCE. The last time . . . Did he stay for the weekend . . ?

MAM. Are you not going to open your present . . ?

GEORGE. I'm opening it . .

MAM. I don't know what your religion is . . But they're the Anti-Christ . . The Communists . . That's why they're losing the war in Russia . . .

GEORGE. They're *winning,* the war, man . . It's all Stalin pulling the wool over Schickelgruber's eyes . . .

MAM. I must say I didn't think you were one of them . .

HELEN. It's not *his* papers, Mam . . .

GEORGE. I'm showing you something . . .

MAM. Are you not going to open yer present . .

GEORGE. I'll bloody *open* it . .

MAM. If that's the way you're going to take it . . Give it me back . . .

GEORGE. I didn't mean that, Peggy . . .

ANDIE. So I goes up to Heaton . . . This wife opens the door . . Cannie . . Clean . . Stone deaf . . . Come in answer to yer advert in the Chronic . . . I says . . . Nice day . . she says . . Her batteries had gone in her deaf aid . . and she was waiting for more to come in . . .

JOYCE. Mam . . I want to know when Eric was last here . . .

MAM. He's *your* bloody husband . . .

GEORGE. *(opening the parcel).* That's lovely . . That . . Ta . . Cannie . . *(Looking at them unsure what they are.)*

MAM. They're cuff links, George . . .

GEORGE. I know what they are . . . Here's a kiss for them . . .

MAM. George, man . . Don't be daft . . Act yer age . . . Where's me calendar . . .

ANDIE. So I writes it down . . . On a pad . . . What I'm doing there . . . Takes a long time to have a conversation writing things down . . .

MAM. What's he talking about? . . Da . . what are you rambling on about . . ?

ANDIE. I'm going to the Heaton widow's . .

MAM. What for? . .

GEORGE. He's telling you . . .

MAM. Eric came on leave from Pickering . . didn't he . . The last time . .
He got his Corporal stripes . . He looked nice in his stripes . . didn't
he, Helen . . . That's right . . . It was a Wednesday, he came wasn't
it . . . Didn't have to go back the same day to Pickering.

JOYCE. Wasn't that the time before, Mam?

MAM. I'm looking . . .

GEORGE. It's a Party card . . . I know what I'm doing . . . My position
on the Shop Stewards' Committee . . . I had to join the party . . .
Peggy . . .

MAM. What's he talking about, now . . .

GEORGE. The Communist Party . . . I'm a Communist . . .

MAM. Sit down a minute, man . . I'm trying to work out when Eric was
here . . What do you want to *know* for anyway . . .

HELEN. She just wanted to know . . .

GEORGE. That's my card . . Everybody in the Yard's joining . . .

MAM. George . . . First thing tonight . . You get to the church . . and go
to confession . . . That's what *you've* got to do . . . God in heaven . .
I can't even have three days away from here . . . without everybody
going mad . . .

ANDIE. I'm just going to the widow's . . . Five shillings a week . . . But I
want my ration books, Peggy . . .

MAM. I went to see Old Mother Riley, at the Gloria . . . That time Eric
was here . . . No . . That was September . . .

HELEN. You might as well hear this, too . . Mam . . . While you're at
it . . .

GEORGE. Helen; Leave her alone, just now . . .

HELEN. Me and Norman . . . Mam . .

MAM. Ee . . You're not . . Thank God . . You're getting married . .
That's lovely . . . I can't believe it . . Norman . . . Come here, pet . . .

HELEN. Mam, man . . . .

ANDIE. I want me ration books, Peggy . . .

MAM. Wait a minute, Da . . I can't get over it . . . Norman . . Helen . .
Do you hear them . . you have all my blessings . . the pair of you . .
I wish you all the happiness in the world . .

HELEN. We're *not* getting married, Mam . . .

NORMAN. Helen . . Do you not think . . you should maybe tell your
mother later . . when . .

MAM. I don't understand you . . Do you understand her, George . . ?

ANDIE. She's not getting married . . .

HELEN. We've got a house . . In Elswick . . A flat . . with a garden . . .

MAM. Helen . . What's the matter with you . . . What are you talking
about . . .

ANDIE. She's got a house in Elswick . . .

MAM. Da . . Keep out of this a minute . . will you . . .

HELEN. I'm thirty-one, Mam . . . I'm old enough to know what I'm
doing . . I'm going to live in Elswick with Norman . . .

MAM. I don't understand her . . I do not understand that girl for one
minute. One minute she's saying she's not getting married, the next
she is . . .

ANDIE. She says . . .

MAM. *You* keep out of this . . .

ANDIE. Give us me ration books then, and I'll get off to Heaton . . .

GEORGE. Andie . . Take it easy . . . Just take it easy a minute . . .
Norman . . . You've lost us here, lad . . . I don't get your drift . . .
I do not get your drift, son . . .

HELEN. It was *my* idea, Da . . . It's no use talking to him . . .

GEORGE. I'm bloody *talking* to him . . . I want something straight . . .
Have you been messing about with . . .

MAM. Don't start acting the father with her after all them years,
George . . Helen, pet . . .

GEORGE. I bloody *am* her father. Am I? Mind *you*. The way things
are going, now I'm not sure . . .

MAM. My God. He's not *married*! He's not a married man, is he?

HELEN. Just fell into it young, Mam. He's not *really* married.

MAM. Oh, dear God in heaven. He's a married man

ANDIE. It doesn't matter, Peggy! . . . It'll all be nothing in a hundred years' time . . .

GEORGE. What the hell good does that do . . . We're bloody here *now*, aren't we, man . . *How's* he not married, Helen?

HELEN. He got married very young . . .

GEORGE. Is he a Russian or something . . Does he have to have an interpreter . .

HELEN. I made up my mind . . To go . . This weekend, Mam . . That's the best thing . . A quick break . . If you can lend us some curtains and blankets . .

GEORGE. You see what you're doing, son . . Do you? . . You're breaking up a whole household . . .

NORMAN. I'm very sorry, Mr. Stott . . . I didn't mean . . .

ANDIE. I'm thinking on . . If this Heaton widow doesn't work out . . . That might be the solution . . If I move in with Helen . . In Elswick . . I like Elswick . . There's cannie fish and chip shops there . . You get the best fish supper in Newcastle in Elswick . .

MAM. I just can't believe it . . George . . I cannot believe it . . It's a nightmare . . The whole thing's a miserable nightmare . . .

HELEN. I'll make you a cup of tea, Mam . . .

MAM. Get your coat on . . We're going round this minute, to Father Kennelly . . .

HELEN. I'm not going anywhere, Mam . . .

GEORGE. If he's getting divorced . . .

NORMAN. There's no divorces during the war, Mr. Stott . . .

GEORGE. *After* the war . . . Before the war . . . If you're getting divorced . .

MAM. What difference does that make . . . What God has joined together, nobody can break asunder . . . You know your Bible as well as me . . .

GEORGE. They haven't that problem in Russia . .

MAM. I'm going to take the pair of you to Father Kennelly's . . .

JOYCE. Take me *too*, Mam . .

MAM. Thank God . . I've at least one good child . . . Come here, pet . . .

GEORGE. I'm just saying . . They have places . . You can get rid of your wife . . at the drop of a hat . . . In Russia . . .

MAM. What do they do . . . Put them down . . Like in the Cat and Dog Home . . . I wouldn't put it past the bloody heathens!

NORMAN. I'm very sorry, Mrs. Stott . . .

MAM. So you bloody should be . . . God in heaven . . We had such a lovely time . . . at Auntie Linda's funeral . . I was so happy . . In the train coming back home . . . And look what I've come back to . . . We've nothing, George . . have we . . . the whole world's collapsed round us . .

HELEN. Mam . . Don't be daft . . There's yer tea, man . .

MAM. How could you do this to us . . Helen . . You were such a good, clean, lovely lass . . . How could you do this to me and your father . . . ?

HELEN. I don't *know*, Mam . . .

MAM. I remember now, Joyce . . . When Eric was last here . . He'd got a lift in a lorry from the camp . . He had to go back the same night . . .

JOYCE *buries her face in her hands.*

HELEN (*to* AUDIENCE). They didn't believe I was going . . Till the Sunday . . When I came into the kitchen . . with my cases and things . . . I felt a bit easier . . because Joyce's period suddenly came . . . It was a false alarm . . . So that was one problem less, me Mam had to face . . .

GEORGE. (*at the piano*).
> You'd be so nice to come home to,
> You'd be so nice by the fire,
> When the breeze on high,
> Sings a lullaby . . . etc.

MAM. Where are you going, pet?

HELEN. Mam . . Don't start that all over again . . .

MAM. Helen . . You can't leave us . . man . . In the middle of a war . . and everything . . Helen . . Pet . .

HELEN. I'll come over and see you every day . . From me work, Mam . . .

MAM. George . . Our lass is going away . . .

GEORGE. It's that bloody Lost Boy's fault . . Bringing the Tailor's dummy home . . . like that . . . Told you . . first time I saw him . . We'll have nothing but trouble from that stupid swine . .

MAM. Are you not even staying for your dinner, pet?

HELEN. I've got to get to the house and arrange everything . .

MAM. I'll never step over your doorstep . . You know that . . . I swear that . . .

HELEN. Ta ra . . Da' . . . Ta ra . . Mam . . . I'm sorry I couldn't have had a nice white wedding for you in St. Anthony's . .

MAM. Don't Helen . . I can't even bear thinking about it . . .

HELEN (to AUDIENCE). I rushed out the house . . Another minute and they'd have me crying too . . . But me Mam came after us . . .

MAM. You forgot yer Ration Book . .

HELEN. Ee . . I did . . .
(To AUDIENCE.) Taking it from her . . . It was a funny feeling . . . Like it was the final break . . from her . . . It was funny taking that ration book . . . It was harder to do than anything I'd done up till then . . .

MAM. Will you go to Mass, tonight . . . For me . . ?

HELEN. Alright . . I'll go . . .

MAM. Is there a shelter in yer place . . ?

HELEN. It's a good one . . Better than ours . . An Anderson . .

MAM. Thank God for that . . !

GEORGE. You'd be so nice to come home to . .
You'd be so nice by the fire . . . . etc.

HELEN (to AUDIENCE). A funny thing happened . . When we were sitting down . . . To our dinner . . Norman had got some haddock . . . One of the lads in the unit had been fishing off the pier . . It was lovely . . . We were just sitting down to have it . . . when the bells started ringing . . All over Newcastle . . .

NORMAN. Did you put it in the Sunday Sun . . . ?

HELEN. I must've done . . . Is it the invasion . . ?

NORMAN. Can't be the invasion, Helen . . They sound too cheery . . . It's a peel . . . They'd be sounding the sirens . . wouldn't they . . .

HELEN (to AUDIENCE). We went outside . . It was cold . . . Norman put his arms around us . . . when he noticed I was shivering . . .

NORMAN. I'll tell you what it's for . . . It's for Tobruk . . . It's victory bells . .

HELEN. Eee . . It is . . Listen to them . . .

(*To* AUDIENCE.) We stood in the doorway . . Listening to the bells ringing out all over Newcastle . . . It was like a sign for me and Norman . . I felt it was . . And it was the first time . . I felt any hope

(*To* NORMAN.) . . I feel that, now . . Do you? . . Things are turning . . . We're going to beat them, at last . . . The Germans . . . We're going to be all right!

NORMAN. It's a good sound that, isn't it . .

HELEN. Come on . . . Our haddock'll be getting cold, love . .

Up 'So Nice to Come Home to'.

Scene Two

The White Cliffs of Dover
6 and 7 June 1944

GEORGE. There'll be bluebirds over,
  The white cliffs of Dover,
  Tomorrow, just you wait and see,
  There'll be love and laughter
  And peace ever after,
  Tomorrow, when the world is free.
  etc . . .

MAM. Helen . . Yer Da's been hit by a bomb . .

HELEN. Eee . . he hasn't, man . . .

MAM. He's in the General . . . I can't face going up to see him on me own . .

HELEN. I was just going to wash me hair, Mam . . Wait — I'll get a coat on . .

MAM. That raid before . . Did you get it . . . Just one bloody plane got through . . . And it had to get your Da . . .

HELEN. I'm just coming, Mam . . .

MAM. To think we've gone all through the war without a scratch . . . And it had to happen now . . . Dear God. Helen . . say your rosary on the way . .

HELEN. I'll say it, Mam . .

(*To* AUDIENCE.) I hadn't got me rosary . . or even me Missal . . . It had got lost years back . . . I don't know what the plane was doing over Newcastle . . It was D Day . . . and you'd have thought the Germans would've needed all their planes over in France . . .

(*To* MAM.) Did they say how bad he was, Mam . . ?

MAM. I didn't dare ask, man . . . I wouldn't care . . But I'd just come in from Mass and Confession . . .

HELEN. I thought he was on day shift, Mam . .

MAM. I'm telling you . . It happened at the Yard . . . Have you got yer torch . . . ? Eee . . When I saw the policeman at the door . . . He was firewatching at the Yard . . It was his night . . . He was a good Da to you . . wasn't he . . Whatever you say about him . . He was a lovely Da . . .

HELEN. He'll be all right, Mam . . .

MAM. And a good man to me . . . Couldn't get a better man . . .

HELEN. Is Joyce at work . . ?

MAM. I don't know where anybody is . . . Dear God . . A thing like that to happen to us . . .

HELEN. It'll be alright, Mam . . .

MAM. How can it be alright . . . For God's sake . . The poor man's been struck by a bomb . . .

HELEN (*to* AUDIENCE). It couldn't have been a very big one . . Because when we got to the hospital . . They told us he'd gone home . .

MAM. Gone home . . . It's George Stott . . .

HELEN. They said that was right . . .

MAM. He's been in an air raid . . . A bomb hit him . . .

HELEN (*to* AUDIENCE). We tried to get a taxi straight back to Walker . . Me Mam was sure they'd made a mistake . . And he'd died on the road . . .

HELEN (*to* AUDIENCE). When we got back . . Joyce was fighting with Eric, who was telling her how he'd lost his stripes . . .

ERIC. I've told you, man . . I was in trouble . .

JOYCE. What trouble . .

HELEN (*to* AUDIENCE). . . . And me Granda had turned up, with his problems . . .

ANDIE. Helen . . I want to talk to you . . . That spare room you've got in Elswick . . .

MAM. Is he not here? . .

JOYCE. Who's not here? . .

MAM. I told you . . didn't I . . They've lost him . . They made a mistake . . and they're trying to cover up . . . Da' . . . He's gone . . He's passed away . . . The Germans got him . . . I've just come from the General . . . A bomb hit him . .

HELEN. Stop panicking . . Mam . . Joyce make a cup of tea . . will you . .

ERIC. You're an old soldier, Andie, . . aren't you? . .

ANDIE. Who's hit by a bomb . . George has never been hit by a bomb, has he? . .

JOYCE. Eee . . He hasn't, has he, Mam?

ERIC. How would he be hit by a bomb, man . . If he was hit by a bomb . . He'd be smashed to smithereens . . Bits of him would be blown across to Gateshead . .

MAM. For God's sake . . Tell your man to hold his rotten tongue . . .

ERIC. I'm just saying . . what would happen if he was hit by a bomb . . amn't I? . . .

JOYCE. Keep quiet, a minute, Eric, man . . .

ANDIE. Didn't you used to be a Corporal . . .

ERIC. Don't *you* bloody start . . .

MAM. He was firewatching . . I gave him spam sandwiches . . . . for his bait . .

ERIC. *I* wouldn't *mind* a spam sandwich . . .

HELEN. Where are you going now, Mam? . . .

MAM. Going back to the General . . To find me man . . . I've got a right to him . . Whatever state he's in . . Put your coat on, Helen . . . .

ERIC. Them hospitals . . Mrs. Stott . . If they said he's gone, he's gone . . They know what they're talking about . . .

MAM. Ee . . That's what's happened . . They said he was gone . . And we thought they meant he'd left the hospital . . Dear God . . .

HELEN. Mam . . They didn't . . They said he'd left the hospital . . To go home . . .

MAM. I don't remember them saying that . . Did they say that? . . They said he'd gone . . .

HELEN. Went home . . .

MAM. Where is he, then, for God's sake?

ERIC. I don't understand anybody going home after a bomb hitting him . . .

JOYCE. You don't understand anything . . . You don't even know how you lost yer bloody stripes . . .

MAM. Where is he? . . . *(Going.)*

ERIC. Where's she going, now? . . .

ANDIE. Going to have a chat with the Virgin Mary . . . Best thing for her . . .

JOYCE. Helen . . Nothing has happened to our Da . . has it? . .

HELEN. Eee . . I don't know, Joyce . . .

ERIC. Did you say you were making a spam sandwich . . .

HELEN. I don't live here now . . . Better ask your wife, Eric? . .

ERIC. God . . I could, Granda . . You'right there . . .

HELEN (*to* AUDIENCE). Then me Dad came in . . . With a bit of sticking plaster at the side of his head . . . Everybody shut up . . . Like a ghost had walked into the room . . . The Old Soldier spoke first . .

ANDIE. It must've been a *smallish* kind of bomb, Geordie . .

MAM. Eee . . George . . Are you alright, pet . . . Where have you been . .

GEORGE. Give us a seat, somebody . . . will you . . . Helen, make us a cup of tea . . .

MAM. Do you want some brandy? . . . We've been all over Newcastle looking for you, pet . . . Haven't we Helen?

GEORGE. I could do with some brandy . .

JOYCE. Are you alright, Da . . .

GEORGE. Three weeks ago . . He knew the clock on Newcastle Town Hall was two minutes slow . . Lord Haw Haw . .

ANDIE. George . . She's getting ideas . . . The Black Widow . .

GEORGE. Two nights ago . . Lord Haw Haw . . Did you hear him? . .

MAM. Is that all they did to you . . . I mean . . Have you any internal injuries, George . . They haven't damaged any of yer insides . . .

GEORGE. He says . . Lord Haw Haw . . 'The Communists and Jews are kidding themselves. Germany's beaten . . . Germany is stronger than ever . . . '

ERIC. Bloody bluff . . You should see the stuff we've been loading (*Stops himself.*) . . . I'm not supposed to say anything about it anyway . . . You didn't hear that . . Did you?

ANDIE. Is that how you lost yer stripes . . .

ERIC. I lost me stripes because they took us for a spy . . .

GEORGE. Do you not want to hear about my encounter with Hitler . . Fair enough . .

MAM. We're listening, man . . But you keep on about bloody Lord Haw Haw . . .

GEORGE. He warned the Communists and the Jews . . to watch out . . . It's well known the Communists are strong in the Neptune Yard . . . We sell more Daily Workers there than anywhere else in the North . .

MAM. May God forgive you . . .

GEORGE. Up Uncle Joe . . Right, Eric?

ERIC. Up the Ruskies . . .

GEORGE. They showed them what for in Stalingrad . . Didn't they . .

MAM. You ask him, Helen . . . Is he damaged inside . . .

GEORGE. I'm telling you, woman . . . I was up there . . . on the roof . . fire watching . . .

MAM. Did you eat yer spam sandwiches . . .

GEORGE. I did, they were very nice . .

JOYCE. Mam . . I want to know how Eric was taken for a spy . .

GEORGE. I'm up there . . That warning sounds . . . Are you listening to us . . . Leave the bottle here, man . . I've had a terrible shock . . .

MAM. I'm just pouring meself one . . .

GEORGE. Now . . . Here's the thing . . . I'm standing up there . . Alert . . Looking out for incendaries . . bombs . .

MAM. I said a special prayer for you at Mass tonight . . Did you know that . . . That's what protected you . . . And I said a prayer over your sandwiches . . .

GEORGE. I'm standing there when in comes this Heinkel . . Right . . .

ERIC. Down in Sussex . . They thought my Tyneside was a German accent . . that's all . . . Okey dokey . . ?

JOYCE. No . . It isn't okey dokey . .

GEORGE. This Heinkel . . You could see him . . He was looking for something . .

MAM. For you . . .

GEORGE. Looking for the *Yard*, man . . . You could see . . He was going backwards and forwards . . . Look . . If they know Newcastle Town Hall clock's two minutes slow . . They'll know all about the whole communist cell in the Yard . . . They might even've been after me as Party Secretary . . . Wouldn't put it past them . . .

ERIC. From up there . . Mr. Stott . . They couldn't make out *who* you were from there . . .

GEORGE. They dived . . I'm telling you . . . A hail of bullets at us . . . They were so low . . I could read the number on the wings . . See that bloody swastika . . . Diving straight at us . . . I threw me stirrup pump at him . . . Take that you bastard . . ! Then I retreated . . Down the ladder . . . Me helmet dropped off . . . In the heat of the fighting . . .

ANDIE. First rule of a soldier . . Hold on to your rifle and your helmet . . .

GEORGE. That's how they got us . . . A bullet bounced off the wall . . Got me here . . See . . .

MAM. Dear God . . Thank you . . Thank you, dear God . . For bringing my man back to us . . I'm going to put thanks to the Secred Heart in the Catholic Herald this week . . I am . .

GEORGE. Stunned us . . . Next thing I knew . . I was in the General . . Some lass putting a plaster on me head . . . I showed the bastards. Eh . . Eric . . son . . .

GEORGE. One thing . . anyway . . son . . . Right . . . Nobody can say, when it's all over, *I* haven't done my bit for the old country . . .

HELEN (*to* AUDIENCE). It would've been alright . . If we'd had out supper and went to bed . . But me Dad had to drag us all out to the pub on Welbeck Road . . to celebrate . . . And that's where the trouble started . . . Eric went for the drinks . . Me Mam and Da' sat at the table . . When he came back . . He had only two pints . . . I

didn't want one anyway . . . As soon as me Mam saw that . . . She
stood up . . Pulled me Da' up too . . . And walked out the pub
without speaking . . .

ERIC. It was queuing up . . Mrs. Stott . . .

HELEN (*to* AUDIENCE). Eric tried to hold her back . . But she was
off . .

ERIC. The chap in front of us . . . I'll get you yer drinks . . . I got mixed
up . . .

JOYCE. Eee . . Eric . . What have you done now . . .

ERIC. I wouldn't deliberately not get yer Mam and Da a drink, Joyce . .
would I . . . Look (*showing them his money*) . . . I've got plenty of
money on us . . .

JOYCE. Where did you get all that . . . ?

ERIC. It was about her . . I was only defending her . . This chap in front
of us . . . He made a nasty remark about yer Mam, man . . I'm telling
you . . .

JOYCE. Like what did he say? . .

ERIC. A nasty remark . . .

JOYCE. Maybe he was a spy like you . . .

ERIC. For Christ's sake . . I'm telling you . . . They did . . bloody think
I was a spy . . . That's how I ended up losing me stripes . . . I got
picked up in Sussex . . At a dance . . That's all . . .

JOYCE. At a *dance?* What were you doing at a dance? . .

ERIC. What do *you* do at a dance . . .

JOYCE. That's what I *mean* . . .

ERIC. You know what it's like . . Before I know it . . . . They've got
this policeman . . And I'm getting the third degree . . who I am . .
and where I come from . . and then the bloody M.P.'s turn up to
take us back to the camp . . Drunk and disorderly . . and losing a
rifle . . I left me rifle in the bog . . That's all that happened . . .

JOYCE. That's all . . You go gadding about looking for lasses in
dances . . while I'm stuck here all on me own . . That's very nice . . .
Now I know where I stand . . .

ERIC. What do you mean . . You know where you stand . . I like
dancing . . You know that . . You don't deny us a bit of a dance
now and then . . *You* know there's no harm in it, Helen . . .

JOYCE. We'd better get back to our Mam, Helen . . .

ERIC. Helen, man . . .

HELEN (*to* AUDIENCE). . . Back in the house . . It was Battle
Stations . . Me mam was sitting there, at the table . . Her arms
folded . . . Black . . . The Coalman was at the piano, hiding from
the storm . . .

ANDIE. I'm just telling yer Mam, Helen . . She wants us to get
married . . . On August Bank Holiday . . . The black widow . .

MAM. I have seen some mean, some miserable characters in my day.. .
But my God! . . . I never thought my own son-in-law —

ERIC. Bloody let us tell you . . .

MAM. Joyce'll tell you . . . Whenever he was due home on leave . . I
saved our meat ration . . . and points . . and everything . . I said:
I want that lad to come home to a decent meal . . I even saved
cigarettes for him . . . Every time he came back, there was twenty
Woodbines on the mantlepiece waiting for him . . . . Is that right,
son?

ERIC. I'm just telling you what happened . . .

MAM. Am I telling you a lie . . . Tonight . . Everybody was having heart
and onion pie . . . What do you sit down to . . .

ERIC. This bloke in the pub . . .

MAM. Pork chop and apple sauce . . . Because I know . . A lad who's
been away fighting for his country wants to come home to a nice,
cheerful, tasty meal . . .

ERIC. Look . . I'm telling you . .

MAM. I was even saving up coupons for his birthday . . Did you know
that, Da?

ANDIE. What you're asking for is people not to be people, Peggy . .
That's where you're falling down . . . Gratitude . . That's not
people . . It would be very nice if people were grateful . . and human
beings and that kind of thing . . But that's not how they're made . . .
People are not human beings . . . That's where you go wrong! . .

MAM. I don't care so much for myself . . But after his wife's father . . .
Has been snatched from the jaws of death . . .

ERIC. It slipped me mind . . in the heat of the minute . . That's all . . .
If you'd have waited another second . . I would've . . .

MAM. I just cannot understand anybody like that . . .

JOYCE. You can stay here and apologise to me Mam . . . But I'm *not* running off with you Eric . . . Not after what I've heard tonight . . . Finding out what you're up to, when you're away from me . . .

ERIC. How do I know what *you're* up to . . like . . When *I'm* away . . . All these bloody Yanks all over the place . . .

JOYCE. What do you mean by that? . .

ERIC. Funny thing . . You're never short of stockings . . are you . . Where do you get them from . . What have you got to do to get them . .

JOYCE. Bloody take that back . . Hear me!

MAM. What are you hinting at, Eric . . .

ANDIE. I must admit . . Peggy . . If I was a lass . . The way them Yanks go about . . Throwing their dollars all over the place . .

MAM. Keep out of this, Da . . Will you . . . Are you insinuating . . .

ERIC. Oh, go and have a shit to yourself . . . The lot of you!

HELEN (*to* AUDIENCE). And he walked out . . . Right out of our lives . . .

ANDIE. Now . . . Eric's not staying . . With me complications with the widow . . You understand . . You think you might take us back for a few weeks . . Till I find somewhere else . . I was going to ask Helen . . But I can't take to Elswick . . somehow . . I mean . . If you've been in Walker all yer life . . . I've nobody to talk to . . in Elswick . . I don't like the library, either . . .

HELEN (*to* AUDIENCE). Joyce . . Stood there . . White . . Looking at the door Eric had gone through . . .

JOYCE. I don't bloody care . . I don't care . . I don't care if he *never* bloody comes back! . . .

GEORGE.   The shepherd will tend his sheep,
           The valley will bloom again,
           And Jimmie will go to sleep
           In his own little room again.

           There'll be bluebirds over,
           The white cliffs of Dover,
           Tomorrow, just you wait and see . . . etc . . .

HELEN (*to* AUDIENCE). On the next morning, the Wednesday, it was on the wireless. They'd landed in Normandy . . They were already miles and miles inside France . . . But all I could think of was

HELEN. Two . . .

NORMAN. Eighteen months or so . . . That week I went back . . It was
a bad week . . Birmingham was really getting it . . . I just went to
see her . . . She was all on her own . . . I mean . . It was me that had
brought her to Birmingham . . She didn't know anybody there . . . I
didn't want to hurt you, love . . .

HELEN. A little boy . . Matthew Peter . . .

NORMAN. *She* named it . . .

HELEN. Do you love him? . . .

NORMAN. I don't know . . . I just felt sorry for her . . . On her own . .

HELEN. So you bloody gave her a kid . . .

NORMAN. I know . . .

HELEN. You *don't* bloody *know* . .

NORMAN. I love you . . . You know that . . . .

HELEN. I don't know anything, Norman . . I know I bloody love
you . . . What did you need to go back to her for . . . Could you not
finish with her . . . Once and for all . . For her sake . . .

NORMAN. You know me . . I'm a bloody idiot . . Amn't I . . . I'm just
one of these characters . . . That mess up their own lives . . . and
everybody that come in contact with me . . .

HELEN. What good does that do . . . Beating your bloody breast about
it!

NORMAN. I love *you*, Helen . .

HELEN. *Do* you? . . .

NORMAN. What do you want to do? . .

HELEN (*to* AUDIENCE). And suddenly . . I felt really weak . . I
hadn't eaten anything all day . . . I suddenly was dying for something
to eat . . . I've got some sausage meat . . .

NORMAN. Yes . . . We'll go home . . .

HELEN (*to* AUDIENCE). I looked at him . . . Trying to get behind
his eyes . . .

NO (*to* NORMAN). Do you love me? . . . I don't *know*, Norman . . .

NORMAN. I *do*, Helen . . .

HELEN (*to* AUDIENCE). There was this scent from the flowers in the
Square . . and the birds were shouting away at the top of their voices . . .

NORMAN. Bloody racket, these birds are making!

HELEN. They do that, before they go to sleep . . .

NORMAN. Do they? . . I'm sorry, love . . I should've told you . .

HELEN. Yes, well . . You couldn't . . No use saying that . . . You couldn't tell us . . .

NORMAN' It just happened . . It doesn't make any difference between us . . . Honest . . It doesn't . . .

HELEN. Doesn't it . . . Come on . . . We'll go back to Clifton Road and have something to eat . . . Before it's time for your train . . .

NORMAN. Do you forgive us . .

HELEN. What does *that* mean?

NORMAN. Do you?

HELEN. I'm not bloody God, am I . . . . Just don't talk about it just now, Norman . . .

(*To* AUDIENCE.) It was such a lovely night . . . Warm . . And all the trees fresh green . . . with their new leaves . . and the birds singing . . And everybody round us happy and full of it . . . And the sight of him . . Looking so miserable . . . dejected . . and guilty . . . I couldn't help it . . .

(*To* NORMAN.) Come here . . You stupid idiot . . . (*Kissing him lightly.*) . . . I still love you . . . I can't help it . . . I wish you hadn't done it but, love . . .

NORMAN. I know . . .

HELEN. You *don't* bloody *know*, Norman . . You don't bloody know the *half* of it, love . . . .

Up 'The White Cliffs of Dover'.

Scene Three

A Nightingale Sang in Berkeley Square
8 May 1945

GEORGE. I'm going to get lit up,
    When the lights go on in London, etc.

The sound of hooters coming from the Tyne . . .

MAM. Look! I got a brown loaf at Jackson's . . .

HELEN (*to* AUDIENCE). The hooters were all screaming away . . . For V.E. Day . . Everybody was smiling and talking to each other in the streets . . . Joyce was sorting out the bunting . . . And me Mam chasing all over Newcastle looking for bread . . .

MAM. Do *you* fancy trying for a loaf, Helen, pet . . .

HELEN. I'll go in a minute . . . Mam . . .

MAM (*to* HELEN). What's he doing there . . . ?

GEORGE. I'm making the guy . . . For the bonfire tonight.

MAM. Is that Hitler?

GEORGE. That's not Hitler . . No . . Hitler's dead . . . Forget about Hitler . . .

MAM. Where did you get that bowler?

GEORGE. It's me old bowler . . . From me wedding . . .

MAM. You're not going to burn that?

JOYCE. What should I do about Eric, Mam?

HELEN. One of these days, Joyce . . . You'll actually make your own mind about something, won't you?

JOYCE. I'm just asking . . .

MAM. Give me that hat . . .

GEORGE. I *need* it . . . That's yer Capitalist . . . You burn capitalism . . . That's the idea . . That's the whole point of the war . . . Isn't it . . Finish the old system . . once and for all . .

JOYCE. Did you read *his* letter?

HELEN. I read his letter . . .

JOYCE. What do you think? You see, he's due in about an hour. Shoud I go and meet him . . ?

HELEN (*to* AUDIENCE). That week . . . Eric had written her . . . First time since he walked out of our house . . .

JOYCE. It was a nice letter, wasn't it . . .

HELEN. Yes . . . It was all right . . .

(*To* AUDIENCE). 'Dear Joyce, I'm coming back from Sussex on eighth at six o'clock . . If you want to meet us at the station . . . Hope you are keeping well . . Eric . . '

He was going to put 'love' . . but you could see he'd had second thoughts . . .

JOYCE. I mean . . . For *Eric* to write a *letter* . . *You* know him, Mam . . .

MAM. Meet.him, if you want to . . Is nobody going out to see if they can get some more bread . . .

JOYCE. Mam . . . You see . . . I thought we were finished . .

JOYCE. Would *you* come with us, Helen? . . .

HELEN (*to* AUDIENCE). Then the Old Soldier turned up . . . with his cat and his gear . . .

GEORGE. Is that cat still living Andy . . . he'll be due his old age pension, now . . . won't he . . .

ANDIE. I'm here . . .

MAM. What's the matter? . . .

ANDIE (*to* GEORGE). How's the Hero, eh . . . ?

GEORGE. I mean . . . You've got to hand it to us . . We've done it haven't we? . .

MAM. Da' . . . What are you doing here, with your cases and Tibbie?

ANDIE. You asked us, woman . . . When I saw you in Shields Road the other day . . . I was touched . . .

JOYCE. I think this time . . If we had a place of our own . . . Like Helen . . . That's what we've got to do . . We're going to find a place . . .

MAM. I meant . . . Come up for a bite or something . . . That's all I meant . . .

ANDIE. I made a mistake . . I'm sorry . .

MAM. It's Eric turning up . . .

ANDIE. Where is he? . .

JOYCE. I'm meeting him at the station, Granda . .

ANDIE. Taking up with him again . . . ?

JOYCE. I don't know . . .

ANDIE. Say you do know, and you'll know. (*Looking at the effigy.*) What the hell's that?

MAM. Well might you ask.

GEORGE. What do you think it is?

ANDIE. Looks like you on yer wedding day.

JOYCE. What do you mean, Granda? Say I know.

ANDIE. I don't know, Joyce. Sometimes I say owt . . First thing that
comes into me head . . It doesn't matter in the end, does it, Joyce?
He's as good as any other lad, isn't he, Eric? I mean . . He has all his
equipment . .

GEORGE. What do you think, Andie . . The dawn of a new world, eh?

ANDIE. Is it?

GEORGE. Wait and see, lad. The people are going to take over the
world they fought for. Right, Joyce?

MAM. I'd *like* you to stay, Da . . Us all under the one roof on V.E.
night . . But it's Eric . . And not having enough bread . . .

ANDIE. I'll get some bread . . . The widow's got bread.

GEORGE. Peggy . . . Give us back me bowler . . . Look . . . Without
the hat . . . It looks nothing . . . Look at it . . .

GEORGE. Peggy, give us back me hat . . .

MAM. Why can't you burn *Hitler* like every other normal person in
the country . . .

HELEN (*to* AUDIENCE). . . . I was meeting Norman at the
Square . . . He was coming back from Durham . . To spend V.E.
night with us . . . We were going to see all the lights . . . and end
up at the bonfire in Walker Park . . .
. . . I was really full of it . . Going to the Square . . . The town
was packed . . . Lasses at times kissing soldiers . . . or airmen . .
and that . . . They were doing something at the top of Eldon
Monument . . Putting up torches or something . . To light at
night . . . There was bunting all over Newcastle . . .
. . On me way in I even got a white loaf for me Mam . . and one
for ourselves . . . I know I was daft . . but that was like a sign . .
Everything was going right for us, at last . . .
. . . I didn't twig at first . . . that Norman was carrying a case . .
I was before him . . at our seat . . . I just saw Norman . . . The
case didn't register . . . Afterwards, I knew he was carrying it,
so that I would see it . . . and it would help him to break it to
us . . . But all I saw was Norman . . .

(*To* NORMAN:) . . . I beat you, love . . .

NORMAN. Yes . . . I've been to the flat . . .

HELEN. Oh . . . Did you go for a shave and that . . .

NORMAN. Helen . . . I've got to go to Birmingham, tonight . . .

HELEN. Sit down a minute . . . Has something happened, love . . .
    There's nothing happened to yer Mam or Da . . Has there?

NORMAN. I'm getting moved to Leicester . . .

HELEN. I brought a flask of tea . . Do you want a cup of tea . . .
    and a biscuit . . .

NORMAN. See . . My mother's in a right state . . with Tony . . .

HELEN (to AUDIENCE). . . There was only two of them . .
    Like Joyce and me . . Tony and him . . . He'd been missing since
    Arnheim . . .

    (To NORMAN:) . . Have they told them definitely . . He's
    been killed . . .

NORMAN. He's had it . . . Helen . . You know that . . . . . You
    know what happened in that bloody mess . . She's in a real
    state . . . I 'phoned them last night . . . I've got leave . . . To go
    to her . . . .

HELEN. You didn't tell us you were applying for leave, love . . .

NORMAN. Compassionate leave . . . I've got ten days . . . and
    they're moving us to Leicester . . That's near . . you see . . .
    To Birmingham . . .

HELEN. Eric's turned up from nowhere . . . Joyce's gone to
    meet him . . .

NORMAN. That's good . . . They'll all be coming back now . . .

HELEN. What time's your train, then . .

NORMAN. Couple of hours . . .

HELEN. You're going to miss the bonfire, then . . and everything . . .

NORMAN (nearly breaking): . . . I know, Helen . . . I'm going to miss
    everything, love . . .

HELEN. What's the matter, pet . . Come on . . What's wrong, . . .
    love . . .

NORMAN. I love you . . .

HELEN. I know . . .

NORMAN. Just . . . I'm getting pulled . . . all ways . . .

HELEN. It'll be all right, love . . . I'll come and see you at Leicester . .
will I? . . . And when you're demobbed . . .

NORMAN. I'm telling you . . That's it . . Helen . . . I don't know if
I'm *coming* back . . . That's what I'm saying . . .

HELEN. You going back to *her* . . . Is that what you mean?

NORMAN. I don't know . . . My mother wants me back . . With what
happened to Tony . . . She wants me near her . . .

HELEN. You going back to *her* . . . Are you? In Birmingham . . ..

NORMAN. It's not that . . .

HELEN. Do you lover *her* better than me . . Is that what you've
found out, Norman?

NORMAN. I don't know what I'm going to do in the end . . .
It's the kid . . . isn't it? . . . I love him . . He really needs me . . .
You should see him . . . When I'm with him . . . I mean . . .
A kid . . he needs a father . . . doesn't he? . . .

HELEN. Yes . . A kid needs a father . . . Yes . . . I suppose he does . . .

NORMAN. In a few months, it'll be clear . . . . . Just now . . . You
don't know where you are . . . do you?

HELEN. I know where I am . . Norman . . Yes . . I do . . . I'm clear
enough . . .

NORMAN. I don't want to leave you, Helen . . I love you . . . You
not see that . . .

HELEN. I don't know what I see, Norman . . . I should've known
that . . . shouldn't I . . . I mean . . I should've known . . we
weren't going to kind of live together for the rest of our lives . . .
I shouldn't have got into thinking like that . . . The two of us
should be together till death parted us . . . That was stupid . . .
wasn't it . . . You've got things pulling you away from us . . All
the time . .

NORMAN. I think . . in the end . . when it's all clear . . I'll come
back to you . . . I'll write to you . . . I'll send you an address
where you can write to me . . .

HELEN. Do you want some tea? I'm having some tea . . . I was
looking forward to walking round the town . . . with all the
lights on . . . with you . . . Your train'll be away . . . won't it . . .
Before it's dark . . . I've a biscuit . . .

NORMAN. I don't want a biscuit . . No . . .

HELEN. I was even thinking . . now the war's finished . . . If I
could have a kid . . .

NORMAN. Helen . . I'm sorry, love . . I bloody am . . .

HELEN. I know . . . It doesn't do any good, does it . . . Me Mam
made them biscuits . . They're horrible . .

NORMAN. Give them to the pigeons . . .

HELEN. What'll we do, till your train's due . . . ?

NORMAN. You're really good . . You deserve somebody really
good . . . Not a useless rotten bastard like me . . .

HELEN. I said . . I do . . . You're right . . . I might go out and look
for somebody now . . . Now I know I deserve somebody
worthwhile . . . If Joyce and Eric take up again . . . Should I give
them the flat . . . ?

NORMAN. I don't know . . love . . .

HELEN. Come on then, Norman . . Cheer up . . We've won the war,
haven't we . . . ?

JOYCE. Helen . . love . . Come here and see what Eric's got for you . . .

HELEN (to AUDIENCE). They were all there . . . the whole
family . . . Me Mam was making up the Old Soldier's bed in the
kitchen . . . Eric was dancing with Joyce . . .

ERIC (with a banana). I've got a present for you . . There you are . . .
Haven't seen one of these for a long time . . . Eh? . . .

HELEN. Ee . . . Where did you get it, Eric . . .

ERIC. Give yer long lost brother a kiss, man . . . Come on . . .
Got it off a lad on the train . . In the Merchant Navy . . .

JOYCE. Give him a kiss, man . . .

ERIC. She's changed . . . Hasn't she . . . Look at her . . . *You* used to
be the bonny one in the family, didn't you, Joyce . . .

HELEN. Don't be daft, Eric, man . . .

ANDIE. Gone to Birmingham . . Has he . . . Norman? . . .

HELEN. His Mam's upset . . . With Tony missing . . .

ERIC (with banana). You know what to *do* with it, do you, Helen?

HELEN. I'm not as green as I was when we started the war, Eric . .
I think so, love . . .

JOYCE. Ee . . . Don't, Helen, man . . . !

ERIC. Are we going to the bonfire, Mrs. Stott?

MAM. Not me . . . I'm not going to any bloody bonfire to show
meself up . . . With all the Fathers watching . . .

GEORGE. Peggy, man . . .

ANDIE. You all right then . . . Helen?

HELEN. I'm cannie . . . Are you?

ANDIE. Never think about it . . . Doesn't matter . . does it? . . .
As good as I'll ever be . . .

ERIC. Come on Mrs. Stott . . . Be a sport . . .

MAM. Not with that bloody communist dummy . . . I am not going . . .

ANDIE. Stick on a label . . 'Lord Haw Haw' and burn that bugger
instead . . .

GEORGE. Five years . . . Bloody fighting for yer freedom . . .

ANDIE. Told ye, didn't I . . . Exactly the same thing in 1918 . . .

HELEN (*to* AUDIENCE). When we went out into the street . . .
Everything was lit up . . . The whole world was lit . . . There was
something burning really bright in the distance . . . I think it was
the flares on the Eldon statue . . .

MAM. Ee . . The lights . . Look at them, Helen . . Love . . . I can't
get over them . . . Can you . . . Listen . . . There's a late mass . . .
tonight . . Will you come with us, love . . .

HELEN. I might do, Mam . . . I might . . .

(*To* AUDIENCE:) . . . Too many things had happened to us . . .
that day . . . I was still drained inside us . . . whenever I thought of
Norman . . . It was like a real pain in my body . . . It stabbed us . . .
Every time I thought of him . . .
They all went back into the house . . . I stood on the pavement
taking everything in . . . The whole of Welbeck Road was a string
of lights . . . People making their way to the Park for the
bonfire . . . Eric called out to us . . .

ERIC. Eh Helen, man. Come and dance with us.

HELEN (*to* AUDIENCE). . . . I was going to say to him . . .
'Eric . . I can't dance' . . Then I remembered I did . . I *could* . .
now . . . And I let him put his arms round us . . . And dance us
away . . .

HELEN (*to* ERIC). . . Eric . . . I really enjoyed that banana . . .

(*To* AUDIENCE:) I really did, too . . .

They all sing 'Roll Out the Barrel'.

The End